Kill the Overseer!

Forerunners: Ideas First

Short books of thought-in-process scholarship, where intense analysis, questioning, and speculation take the lead

FROM THE UNIVERSITY OF MINNESOTA PRESS

(Continued on page 92)

Kill the Overseer!
The Gamification of
Slave Resistance

Sarah Juliet Lauro

University of Minnesota Press

MINNEAPOLIS
LONDON

Some discussions of the Assassin's Creed games presented here appeared in "Digital Saint-Domingue: Playing Haiti in Videogames," *Small Axe: Archipelagoes* 2 (September 2017), http://smallaxe.net /sxarchipelagos/.

Published by the University of Minnesota Press, 2020
111 Third Avenue South, Suite 290
Minneapolis, MN 55401-2520
http://www.upress.umn.edu

Available as a Manifold edition at manifold.umn.edu

The University of Minnesota is an equal-opportunity educator and employer.

Contents

Videogames as Commemoration

WHEN I TELL PEOPLE that I'm working on a project concerning videogames about slave revolt, the response is almost always one of surprise that such things exist. And I'm not speaking here of figurative representations, such as when an alien race enslaves humanity or a serving class of androids revolt. I'm looking specifically at digital games about historic transatlantic slavery and the strategies of resistance employed by the enslaved—games with badges for disobeying the master and points for freeing slaves and where an adventurous quest has been made of the journey of the fugitive following the north star to freedom. In some of these games, as the title suggests, the player must "kill the overseer" to advance.

Digital, interactive narratives may seem like a suspect medium in which to translate the experience of enslavement and resistance because of their association with entertainment and leisure and because of the poor optics of an enslaved person being reduced to an object directed by the player, whether the visual representation is literalized in a realist manner, or abstracted and suggested by a blinking dot traversing a plantation landscape, or never shown because the play is rendered in the first person point of view. Nonetheless, it seems productive that digital narratives can place limits on their own interactivity and thereby acknowledge the insufficiency of the medium to represent the particular historical trauma of transatlantic slavery.

Recently someone asked me if videogames can do anything that books can't. Why, she asked, should we study videogames on this delicate subject matter, slave resistance? As this Forerunner will enumerate, videogames can enrich our complex relationship to the subject matter because, unlike a book, they are capable of resisting the player. Imagine, I found myself saying to her, if you picked up a book and were reading the story of a rebel slave, but, at a certain point, the pages fought back against you: *imagine that the page refused to be turned*. Imagine if, at other points, you needed a password to reveal a passage. Imagine that you needed to prove to the text your worthiness to read it by solving a puzzle. Imagine if, after all of that, the ending erased itself, refusing to be legible. If the text could refuse admittance to the reader it would, firstly, parallel the themes of resistance and revolt described in the narrative. But secondly, and more importantly, it could underline the difficulty of our apprehension of the historic subject matter.

The recalcitrant text could point to the problems that exist with our historical record, as one kept by the oppressor, in the plantation ledger and the ship captain's logs and bills of sale and notices posted for the recapture of runaways. The defiant book might resist contemporary readers' consumption of the narrative as entertainment and prompt them to question their own investment in the character whose plight they are following. The obstinate narrative might mirror our culture's resistance to memorializing rebel slaves in the same way that we laud other types of freedom fighters. But equally, such a book could respond differently to each reader, letting some pass to the next chapter where others were blocked, suggesting that some will have a different relationship to the material than others. The book's intractability could be used to emphasize the historical distance between the contemporary reader and the person for whom enslavement was a reality. Finally, defying my easy translation to the simile of a book that refuses to be read, the videogame can operate as a meta-critique of its own form. In brief, it can call into question whether such important historical narratives *should* be translated into an interactive form at all.

Like most people of my generation, I grew up playing Nintendo and PC computer games—in the Ivory Coast in the late eighties and Morocco in the early nineties—but I have never been a gamer. My work to date, even when it was on zombies, has mostly sidestepped the medium of videogames for the simple reason that I'm not very good at them. But I could not ignore these texts as objects of study when I discovered them because I am in the process of developing a longer monograph on commemorations of slave resistance. I'm particularly invested in those games that use a poetics of absence, what I'm calling here "the gap," to foreclose the player's complete immersion in the fiction, underscoring the problematics of the form's interactivity and the illusory nature of the player's occupation of the position of the rebel slave. Aside from my interest in what role the form of a videogame could play in enriching our relationship to the content, two questions motivated my interest in these digital texts, and the first was whether or not they could be considered "alternative monuments."

Whereas many nations in the hemisphere (like Barbados, Brazil, Cuba, Guadeloupe, Guyana, Haiti, and Jamaica) have long celebrated histories of slave resistance in the public square, our own landscape in the United States is pocked with confederate memorials, and debate continues to rage about which histories are worthy of commemoration. Though we have memorials to abolitionists like Frederick Douglass and Sojourner Truth, it is rare to find statues commemorating violent freedom fighters in the United States, and even the placement of historical markers has been protested at some sites, like the Great Dismal Swamp where Nat Turner purportedly hid after his rebellion. In contrast, one of the leaders of the Haitian Revolution, Jean-Jacques Dessalines, who ordered the execution of every white man, woman, and child in the French colony that would become a sovereign nation, is honored in countless public memorials that stand watch over a country founded by the descendants of rebel slaves.

To get a sense of the disparity between our acknowledgment of resistance as compared to that of other nations, we might subtract the number of memorials from the number of known incidents of slave rebellion. Here's an extreme case: it is estimated that there were uprisings on one in every ten slave ships. David Richardson, director of the Wilberforce Institute for the study of Slavery and Emancipation, counts 392 events of armed resistance against captors, with twenty-two foiled plots and still more attacks of slave ships by Africans ashore.[1] And yet, there is only one memorial to shipboard slave revolts in the United States, the Amistad memorial in New Haven, Connecticut. Traveling in Haiti while writing my first book, I wondered, "where are *our* monuments to slave revolt, and if they aren't, as in other countries, found in the public square, then are they to be found in other forms?" In brief, because mainstream U.S. culture is unwilling to celebrate slave resistance in the form of statuary and monuments, I wanted to explore media where this work was being done. It often falls to the arts to make up for this dearth, and works like performance artist Dread Scott's 2019 slave revolt reenactment, Kerry James Marshall's 2012 portraits of the leaders of the Stono Rebellion, and Colson Whitehead's 2016 fantastical novel *Underground Railroad* reckon with this void.

The larger project that I am working toward will address material monuments that exist elsewhere in the Atlantic world, as well as alternative monuments to slave resistance in various forms, including the visual arts, literature, film, digital media like videogames and online resources, and memorialization in museums and upon historical sites. In particular, I'm interested in highlighting a productive use of absence in these commemorations. In a longer book project, I'll attend to the work of memorializing and remembering, engaging specifically with theories of public memory more broadly, including how absences, lacks, and silences have been used to represent cultural trauma, as in Holocaust memorials. But I'll also consider whether an absence of a monument can be considered an alternative monument.

Can monuments take other forms, including, even, the destruction of other monuments? Is the pulling down of a confederate statue by a group of protestors one of these "alternative monuments to slave resistance," as I began calling them? Was one of

1. See abolitionproject.org and David Richardson, "Shipboard Revolts, African Authority, and the Atlantic Slave Trade," *William and Mary Quarterly* 58, no. 1 (January 2001): 69–92.

them the destruction of a stained-glass window depicting slaves that a janitor on the Yale campus had purposefully broken?[2] Is the blank plane of glass that was installed in its place a monument to the cultural trauma of slavery and even, perhaps, a lament for our lack of memorials to slave resistance? If, in thinking about the gaps in our cultural landmarks as a kind of indicator, we make the immaterial material, that is, we take their absence as a thing worth thinking about, then we should also consider how absences within texts about slave resistance are themselves legible as signifiers. Indeed, the gap, the break, the blank space observed in many texts about slave resistance is a feature I want to read.[3] In some places, lack may be a nod to the absence of concrete memorials. In others, it may be an acknowledgment of the non-status of the enslaved person. I want to stare not *into* the void, but *at* it.

In this study of videogames that depict strategies of resistance to transatlantic slavery, what I'm calling "the gap" creates a space to acknowledge the limitations of the text. In other places, I've written about the use of the gap to critique the archive and to highlight our dependency on a history written primarily by the slaveholder, where slave resistance is demonized when it is noted at all. The part of my research that I present here is my assessment of the role of silence, gaps, aporias, interruptions, fissures, and obstructions in the depiction of a historical reality that is problematically translated into a *playable* form.

I said earlier that two questions motivated my initial interest in these digital texts. My first concerned whether or not such games could be considered alternative monuments to slave revolt; my second query interrogates the problematics of rendering this history of

2. For the backstory on this incident, see Chandelis R. Duster, "Yale Janitor's Act of Civil Disobedience a Stand against Racism," NBC News, July 19, 2016, https://www.nbcnews.com/news/nbcblk/yale-janitor-s-act-civil -disobedience-stand-against-racism-n610416.

3. This is not like Fred Moten's "break" but more like musical rest. Fred Moten, *In the Break: The Aesthetics of the Black Radical Tradition* (Minneapolis: University of Minnesota Press, 2003).

resistance *playable*. Diverse kinds of digital games can be counted among this cache: educational programs aimed mostly at children, with varying levels of interactivity and narrative, art games that we might consider among those "serious games" increasingly studied by videogame scholars, and major titles released for entertainment purposes, in which the player has direct control over slaves in revolt. The games defy easy categorization, as an art game may be more educational than an educational game, and an entertainment commodity might not entertain at all. But for the sake of the organization of this text and its readings of different types of games, I'll rely, in part, on this inadequate taxonomy.

Some games invite the player to inhabit or control a runaway slave who is specifically based on the historical subject of the transatlantic slave trade while others aimed at mature audiences encourage the player to directly oppose and obstruct the mechanisms of the institution, for example by killing slavers and setting their human cargo free. In investigating the forms digital commemorations of slave revolt take, one aspect to be aware of is the level of engagement and interactivity they permit. Is the resisting slave fetishized? Is the avatar reduced to a commodity? The stakes of gamifying the historical rebel slave of the Americas is a vital part of this discussion. One issue that animates this study concerns the catharsis for the player or if, as an article profiling the last game I'll discuss here suggests, such games foster empathy for the enslaved.[4]

I want to make it clear at the outset that empathy is and always has been a tricky issue in the consideration of narratives about the enslaved. In *Scenes of Subjection,* Saidiya Hartman gestures to "the assimilative character of empathy" in melodramas and abolitionist texts. The authors appealed to the readers to feel for the en-

---

4. See Stephanie Carmichael, "Empathy Game *Thralled* Explores Slavery through Love and Motherhood, not Violence," *Venturebeat,* March 19, 2014, https://venturebeat.com/2014/03/19/thralled-empathy-game -ouya/.

slaved by performing an act of substitution, imagining themselves in the other's place.[5] This unfortunate operation is seen today in museum exhibits, such as when slave irons are displayed and patrons are invited to feel the heft of them, a larger phenomenon I've shorthanded with the phrase "Feel the Weight of these Chains," in reference to a display at the London Museum of the Docklands exhibit, *London, Sugar, and Slavery*.[6] It would be better, I would argue, to leave on these walls a blank space for the patron to wrestle with the incomprehensibility of the slave's condition and the unfathomable choice to resist enslavement at considerable risk. My ultimate concern is not with how these games invite the player to incarnate the rebel slave, either to produce empathy or to wrestle with the past, but with how they productively *block* identification with the rebel slave.

This study includes most, but not all, of the videogames I've found in which a player is invited to play at slave resistance.[7] The games profiled here make use of various techniques I'm gesturing to under the umbrella term "the gap," devices that highlight the insurmountable distance between the contemporary gamer and the historical enslaved person in productive ways. There are many questions, which may only be raised at present, that demand a more substantive treatment by videogame scholars attuned to the

5. Saidiya Hartman, *Scenes of Subjection: Terror, Slavery, and Self-Making in Nineteenth-Century America* (Oxford: Oxford University Press, 1997), 21, 35.

6. See Sarah Juliet Lauro, "Feel the Weight of These Chains," *Commemorating Slave Resistance* (blog), https://slaveresistance.tumblr.com/.

7. One game not addressed here is *Playing History: Slave Trade*. The game was lambasted for a scene in which the player had to stack bodies in a slave ship in a manner similar to the game *Tetris*. The backlash, in which journalists took to calling the game "Slave Tetris," forced the game manufacturer to remove the scene in question, but the rest of the game is still highly offensive and not worthy of a lengthy discussion. See Dexter Thomas, "I Played 'Slave Tetris' so Your Kids Don't Have To," *Los Angeles Times*, September 7, 2015.

complexities of the mechanisms of play and ludic operations' delicate control of the relationship between the player and the game. But I am not the person to take on this project. As a cultural historian with experience attending to the ways that the history of the transatlantic slave trade has been encoded in myth (specifically, in the figure of the zombie), my goal here is to provide a survey of some of the representations of slave resistance that I've encountered in a digital, playable form and to investigate how the poetics of such game narratives, and, specifically, the poetics of absence, limit the player's role as a means of safeguarding the ineffable, the inexpressible, the unrepresentable nature of this history.

Bearing in mind both Michel-Rolph Trouillot's acknowledgment that "any historical narrative is a particular bundle of silences"[8] and Saidiya Hartman's discussion of the historical personage's "right to obscurity,"[9] I observe the gap in these digital commemorations of slave revolt as productive spaces. These are found in an encounter with the digital that highlights, rather than seeks to fill, silences, lacks, and fissures. Moments of obstruction of the player's absorption in the narrative (the blocked circuit, the closed path, the interruption, the failed challenge) work against the appropriation of the enslaved avatar just as a glitch, an interruption of the fiction, or a sudden perspectival shift serves to remind the player of the insurmountable distance between himself and the historical enslaved person. These devices are not unique to this genre; rather, I'm arguing that commonplaces of videogames as a form take on new resonances in games about historical slavery because they enrich our understanding of our relationship to the politically fraught matter of historical slave resistance.

By investigating the *form* of digital interactive narratives, such games show us how we see ourselves in relation to the history of slavery and slave revolt. This seems a particularly topical issue giv-

8. Michel-Rolph Trouillot, *Silencing the Past: Power and the Production of History* (Boston: Beacon Press, 1995), 27.
9. Hartman, *Scenes of Subjection,* 36.

en recent events, in a time when "allowable" and "unallowable" forms of black resistance, the value of black lives, and the role of white allies have become central features of political debate. As we'll see, the most effective of these games highlight the difference between playing *at* resistance and doing the work of resistance in the real world. The empty places where our monuments to rebel slaves should be speak volumes about the enduring legacy of slavery in U.S. culture. Digital representations of this history in game form draw on a semiotics of obstruction, absence, blockage, and aporia to leave open a space for what cannot be said; they speak of the horrors of the transatlantic slave trade and anticipate a future, as yet unarrived and perhaps unimaginable, when we will have fully reckoned with the past.

Nat Turner and Harriet Tubman

ALTHOUGH HARRIET TUBMAN ranks among the top ten most recognized figures of American history, what most people know about her is the legend and not the reality of her lifelong work in the antislavery movement, the Civil War, and the struggle for equal rights.[1] I began with a claim that the United States displays a visible discomfort with commemorations of slave revolt, and, in the wake of increased attention to confederate monuments, many others have noted this contradiction.[2] Yet, memorialized in two public sculptures, in Boston and New York, Harriet Tubman may be our national icon of the resistive slave. As an embodiment of the Underground Railroad, Tubman is often the synecdoche by which we can openly talk about slave resistance without having difficult conversations about the white casualties of violent slave revolts.

In the United States, overtly violent rebel slaves like Nat Turner remain highly divisive. In 1831, Turner led an uprising in Southampton, Virginia, that would swell to (by some accounts) over eighty rebels, attacking various plantations across the region and resulting in the assassination of fifty-one white slaveholders and their family members. As is noted in the documentary *Purge This Land* (2017), efforts to place historical markers at the sites

---

1. See Lois E. Horton, *Harriet Tubman and the Fight for Freedom* (New York: Bedford St. Martins, 2013) and Jean M. Humez, *Harriet Tubman: The Life and the Life Stories* (Madison: University of Wisconsin Press, 2003).

2. See Petula Dvorak, "America's Missing Slave Memorials: It's Time to Truly Acknowledge Our Bloody Past," *Washington Post,* August 28, 2017; Kiratiana Freelon, "Look at All These Monuments from around the World That Honor Those Who Fought against Slavery," *The Root,* August 24, 2017; and Samuel Sinyangwe, "I'm a Black Southerner. I Had to Go Abroad to See a Statue Celebrating Black Liberation," *Vox,* August 17, 2017.

important to Turner's revolt, including the cave where he hid—
evading capture after the revolt for more than three weeks—have
been resisted on the grounds that this "terrorist" should not be
commemorated in any way. As can be seen in comments sections
and the talkback pages of historical websites devoted to Turner's
revolt, the execution of women and children during the rebellion
remains a bone of contention. Instead, Turner is memorialized in
diverse forms, like Kyle Baker's graphic novel adaptation of the
highly dubious "historical document" *Nat Turner's Confessions*
and Nate Parker's 2016 film *Birth of a Nation*. Nonetheless, it is
plain that, in the United States, discomfort persists with strategies
of slave resistance that resulted in the bloodshed of white people,
particularly of those who were *complicit* in the mechanisms of oppression rather than its direct operators, like the wives and especially children of slave owners. In the United States it is Tubman,
rather than Turner, who represents the history of slave resistance
in a multitude of forms, including the type of digital narratives I'll
profile here.

The first exhibit on our tour of digital, interactive narratives
about slave resistance is a spate of educational games that seek to
inform schoolchildren about the horrors of slavery and the self-
emancipation of the enslaved. Some readers might have hazy
memories of a 1992 game called *Freedom!* that was created by the
same company that produced the widely known *Oregon Trail,* the
Minnesota Educational Computing Consortium (MECC). In the
game, the player steers a runaway slave either northward or toward an Indian Reservation to seek freedom, confronting various
challenges such as slavecatchers, hunger, and natural obstacles.
The player's success in this mission will depend on the slave's
skills, which appear to be randomly determined by the computer, including literacy and the ability to swim, as well as diligence
in the first level on the plantation, in which the player can amass
various objects to help with the quest and key pieces of advice
from "Elders." Although *Freedom!* doesn't appear to have attained
the level of popularity of some of MECC's other offerings, it may

have left its stamp on a cache of more recent productions aimed at schoolchildren that were created in a similar vein. There are hints that the playable character of *Freedom!* may be able to fight back against the slavecatcher, and he or she can obtain a butcher knife from a house-slave in the first level, but I personally have had little success initiating any play that didn't involve running or hiding, nonviolent means of escape. This seems to be true of these educational resources more broadly: they may enumerate various resistive strategies, but they privilege the nonviolent option of flight from the plantation as the player's central quest. As such, these games are much more in the sphere of Harriet Tubman rather than Nat Turner.

For example, in an online Scholastic resource called "The Underground Railroad: Escape from Slavery," a text box in a supplemental slideshow includes a picture of Nat Turner's arrest, though the accompanying text does not mention him or his rebellion specifically. It reads: "Sometimes [enslaved people] acted out with force, leading revolts, burning crops, and even poisoning their masters." It adds, "They fought back in more subtle ways, too. Some simply worked slowly, quietly damaged property, or took goods from their owners." This passage acknowledges that escaping slavery was but one of the many ways that enslaved people resisted their lot on a scale from armed revolt to feigned ineptitude. Although the information is delivered here without judgment, Turner's revolt is not mentioned directly in the text, and that is telling. The majority of this Scholastic resource, including printables for teachers and other exercises, privileges narratives of flight, and several similar pedagogical resources feature Tubman. Because educational games often put the player in the role of the historical enslaved person, it is perhaps too obvious why Tubman is the preferred representative, but the issue of what level of interactivity is permitted to the schoolchild is also at issue.

The central feature of the pedagogical resource described above, "The Underground Railroad: Escape from Slavery," is a simple, semi-interactive Flash animation consisting of historical photographs with an accompanying narrative about a young, skilled woodworking slave named Walter who chooses to flee enslavement. The story includes an option to have the story read aloud, and the images are dotted with hyperlinks to other resources and teacher activities. This digital narrative differs from the others I'm examining here because the student is put neither in a position of power over the runaway slave's decision-making process, nor is she explicitly occupying Walter's perspective through the use of subjective camera angles or narrative positioning. Interactivity is limited to clicking certain designated spots on the image to bring up windows with further information, like historical images, bits of slave narratives, and even mini-slideshows with additional information (including the image of Turner's arrest). The banner on the top of the screen consists of several tabs: "Begin the Journey," "On the Plantation," "Escape!," "Reaching Safety," "Reaching Freedom," and "Tell the Story." There is a spectrum of playability in this type of educational resource that ranges from those that directly put the student in the position of controlling a runaway slave to those that merely encourage interaction with a set narrative. This Flash animation's limited interactivity and positioning of the interlocutor as a spectator of Walter's story situates it at the lower end of the spectrum, but the rhetorical injunction of the tabs, with verbs like "begin," "escape," and "reach," invites the student to become a participant in Walter's journey. The lone exclamation point after the word "Escape!" is similar to the tone of interactive narratives that hail the student to play *as* the resistive slave, in games both real and imagined.

A 2009 web animation by Brad Neeley called "American Moments of Maybe" darkly imagines an alternative. Dramatizing an advertisement for a videogame based on the real life slave revolt led by Nat Turner in Southampton, Virginia, in 1831, part one of the animation depicts children playing a violent console videogame called "Nat Turner's Punchout," with the tagline, "Make It to the Whitehouse and You Fucking Win the Game." Points are allocated for freeing enslaved friends and for stabbing a white man in the neck with a pitchfork. Advertised in the animation as "The Game about Freedom!" and "The Game that Makes History Come Alive!," Neely's animation lambastes the tastelessness of the industry, and it seems eerily prescient when compared to some recent games created by videogame manufacturer Ubisoft that we will attend to later in this volume.

A detailed analysis of this fragment of a web comic is not needed here, but Neeley's parody provokingly asks questions that are pertinent to the study of interactive narratives about slave resistance, which can only be suggested here for future study: What kind of catharsis is offered the player through his or her ability to remediate slave revolt through play? How is emotional investment and, in particular, empathy created or, importantly, *refused* by the mechanisms of play? To what extent do games about slave resistance commoditize the darkest parts of our history, including the commodification of fellow humans? Does the digital rendering of the history of the transatlantic slave trade in games speak back to the origins of digitality, in the account books and shipping logs of those who transported human cargo?

On this last point, as I have argued elsewhere, the medium of the digital might be the most productive location to reckon with our culture being built atop the foundation of transatlantic slavery. As Jonathan Beller writes, "What happens in the digital ether is not, as we have been sold, immaterial, fully abstract, or free, but rather ineluctably linked to the material conditions of the infosphere's emergence and sustenance."[3] Beller asserts that the digital form is inherently based on the type of data collection preserved in slave ship cargo logs and in plantation account books, which first reduced human beings to a series of ones and zeroes.[4]

3. Jonathan Beller, *The Message Is Murder: Substrates of Computational Capital* (London: Pluto Press, 2018), 20. See also my forthcoming article "Digital Commemorations of Slave Revolt," *History of the Present* 10 (October 2, 2020), which discusses this in more detail.

4. Beller, *Message Is Murder,* 20.

Suffice it to say here that, overwhelmingly, digital resources that invite student participation emphasize *escape* above other forms of resistance, highlighting Tubman's history rather than Turner's. Of particular interest to my study is the use of perspective, the foreclosure of interactivity, and moments when games defy expectations to highlight the separation between the player and the character. The next section profiles several games at this level, those aimed at schoolchildren, asking what type of interactivity is afforded the player and interrogating what effect (and affect) the player's limitations achieve in rendering history playable.

Paths to Freedom

IN A FIRST PERSON PERSPECTIVE GAME created by National Geographic for the iPad called *Underground Railroad: Journey to Freedom,* the playable character, who is never named or shown to lend to the student's immersion in the game, runs away from a Maryland tobacco plantation with a friend called Amos, meeting Harriet Tubman on the way. The gameplay features 3D animation, and the mechanics of play mostly involve mousing over objects and clicking dialog boxes as the player makes choices to advance a successful escape. While the first part of the game mentions the difficulty of toiling in the fields, the threat of the lash, and the fact that the playable character's mother was recently sold off, none of this is depicted visually. The game's focus feels like it is on the thrill of escape, on the choices faced (like whether to take the river or the road), and on the application of objects in the playable character's bindle (like forged papers or a pocket knife) to challenges that reveal themselves. If the playable character gets caught by slavecatchers, he or she is returned to the plantation and sold further south. If wise choices are made, in addition to well-known figures like Tubman and Frederick Douglass, the player and Amos are introduced to other abolitionists like Thomas Garrett, William Still, and Jermain Wesley Loguen as they journey north to Canada; as such, the game clearly has educational aspirations. Though it is possible to get caught and return to bondage, *Journey to Freedom* offers two paths to freedom, one in which the playable character stays and works with Frederick Douglass, eventually buying his or her freedom, and another in which he or she successfully escapes to Canada. But importantly, the game concludes, "You've come to the end of this journey" and offers a "Play Again" button no matter the outcome—whether the playable character is returned to en-slavement or escapes and attains freedom—suggesting that this is a game that cannot be won.

The use of the first person perspective is a common choice for digital activities of this variety, but identification with the enslaved person is engineered through diverse means in other games. The Flash animation game *Following the Footsteps* on the website Pathways to Freedom: Maryland and the Underground Railroad, for example, draws upon the second-person address. *Following the Footsteps* appears to be geared to the young child; it is written at an elementary reading level, with simple imagery and passages read aloud. Early on the narrative explains the daily lot of the slave child with whom the player is called to identify: "You spend most of your days in the big house, doing chores like hauling firewood and taking care of the master's children. They can play whenever they want. But you can't. You have to work." The appeal to empathy is obvious here. "You" are told that your family has died, and only one brother and one sister remain with you. After construct-ing a narrative conflict in which the slaves are being sold off, the game forces the player to make the first of several choices: do you want to stay on the plantation with your brother, or run away with your sister? Decisions are selected by clicking on either side of a divided screen, depicting the outstretched hand of one sibling and a palm calling for pause, respectively. If the player opts to stay with the brother, they are subsequently sold away from each other, and the story ends. If the player goes with the sister, the narrative continues, providing more choices, such as whether to hide during the day or continue the journey in daylight. The game highlights the historical reality of family separation by presenting the player with a heart-wrenching choice.

In contrast to the colorful animation of the National Geographic game but similar to Walter's story in the previous example from the Scholastic website, "The Underground Railroad: Escape from Slavery," the visuals in *Following the Footsteps* are black-and-white photographs, lending to the realism of the narrative. Some of the photos are grainy and appear historical, while others are artistic recreations fabricated for the game that incorporate simple animations, such as silhouettes or words that flow across the screen. The photos themselves make effective use of light and shadow and depth of field; objects are often out of focus or cropped strangely. We see a pair of feet walking in the sand in one, a person's face and hands clasped in prayer in another. In most places, there is just a still, black-and-white photograph and the text box to the left of it, creating a hauntingly spare aesthetic. In some cases, though, the player can mouse over objects in the picture to bring up text boxes with more information, revealing the story behind things like the significance of the big dipper constellation, called "the drinking gourd" by the narrator, the use of a lantern in a window to indicate a safehouse for runaways on the Underground Railroad, and hidden messages acting as signifiers in quilt patterns. We are told, for example, that the enslaved used the monkey wrench pattern to signal an eminent escape attempt.

Following the Footsteps is a serious, somewhat interactive narrative; suiting the subject matter, its feel is pervasively heavy. The home screen depicts the game title accompanied by striking audio: a woman singing a spiritual, "Steal Away to Jesus," a cappella. Unlike the flat narration of Walter in the previous example, the tone of voice in which an actress reads these passages is plaintive and poignant. Although the production values seem comparable to the interactive educational activity on the Scholastic website, with black-and-white photography, player motion limited to cursor control, and voice-over narration, the use of the second person address along with the player's limitation highlight a purposefully frustrating affect for the player situated in the protagonist's place.

In an article called "Just Gaming: Allegory and Economy in Computer Games," Julian Stallabrass reiterates what many videogame scholars (like Sid Meier, Ian Bogost, Alexander Galloway, and Jesper Juul) have stated previously regarding the strict regimentation of the player's conformity to rules as the chief mechanism of gameplay: "In computer games, the player not only identifies with the image but controls it in conformance with strict rules of conduct (or else!): conformity has been extended from assent to action."[1] For Stallabrass, "the goal is utter illusionism . . . and an ever greater immersion in the unreal," but I'm arguing here that games about slave resistance work by emphasizing a frustrating breakdown of the player's expectations of the medium, highlighting the player's separation from the lived historical reality of the playable character.[2]

Gameplay frustration is a common device, however. Gilleade and Dix identify videogame frustration as "that which arises when the progress a user is making toward achieving a given goal is impeded."[3] Though these scholars argue that frustration "is a negative emotion," they identify two different types: at-game and in-game frustration. They identify in-game frustration as resulting from "a failure to know how a challenge is to be completed . . . as when an objective is not given," whereas "at-game frustration arises from a failure to operate the input device . . . in a manner that would give the player the potential to progress." Neither of these categories seems to entirely encompass the type of frustration elicited by these types of digital narrative, however, where the lack of choice

1. Julian Stallabrass, "Just Gaming: Allegory and Economy in Computer Games," *New Left Review* (March–April 1993), https://newleftreview.org/issues/I198/articles/julian-stallabrass-just-gaming-allegory-and-economy-in-computer-games. On choice and limitation in videogames, see Ian Bogost, *Persuasive Games: The Expressive Power of Videogames* (Cambridge, Mass.: MIT Press, 2007) and *How to Do Things with Videogames* (Minneapolis: University of Minnesota Press, 2011); Alexander Galloway, *Gaming: Essays on Algorithmic Culture* (Minneapolis: University of Minnesota Press, 2006); and Jesper Juul, *Half-Real: Videogames between Real Rules and Fictional Worlds* (Cambridge, Mass.: MIT Press, 2011).

2. Stallabrass, "Just Gaming."

3. Kiel M. Gilleade and Alan Dix, "Using Frustration in the Design of Adaptive Videogames," *ACE 2004,* Proceedings of the 2004 ACM SIGHI International Conference on Advances in Computer Entertainment Technology, 228–32.

and mobility departs from traditional expectations of the medium for the deeper purpose of historical reflection. Nonetheless, their description of at-game frustration is useful here:

> at-game frustration is similar to the concept of breakdown in the user-interface design. The concept of breakdown stems from Heidegger and relates to that moment when a tool in some way ceases to be invisible, instead of invisibly being used to accomplish a purpose it becomes the focus of attention. In a computer system when the user has to focus on the interface rather than the task at hand this is breakdown. In "work" interfaces this breakdown is always viewed as bad, however, in playful or ludic designs breakdown may be deliberate in order to encourage reflection or experimentation.

The games I'm interested in defy player expectation, permanently inhabiting the space of the breakdown, in order to force the player to reflect on his or her position in relation to the historical subject of the resistive slave. Setting up player identification with the character, the game mechanics then thwart expectations of the interactive text's function, making the game visible as an object, one that productively illustrates the separation of the player from the playable character.

In *Following the Footsteps,* aside from the few moments where the player is given a choice to make between two options to advance the narrative, the only option is to click the button labeled "Next" (or "Previous" to revisit the last slide). The game emphasizes the weight of choice by dividing a screen down the middle when the player is presented with a dilemma, and it highlights the lack of options in other cases, such as when the player must explore the visual space to discover where images can be interacted with and where they are inactive. Thus, the game puts the player in the position of the slave narratively and visually, and the game mechanics also seem to parrot this by placing limits on the player's control. This is not to say, however, that the game achieves a ludic approximation of the enslaved person's lack of choice—firstly, such a position would risk undermining the agency of the slave, and secondly, we need to be mindful of the fact that, as Stallabrass cautions, "The labour forced on the player is not real."[4] By addressing how digital games allegorize economy, Stallabrass argues that computer games blur "the use of people as instruments in the world and in the game. . . . Computer games perform simulated acts of reification where slices of immaterial code act as living beings arranged and treated as objects." However, we must ask how this function is affected when the commodity referent is the human commodity of the transatlantic slave trade. I would argue that rather than creating an immersive illusion, at-game frustration works in these instances to highlight not only the historical reality behind the game but also the insufficiency of the medium to translate this into gaming form.

Can any contemporary artwork—cinematic, literary, visual, or performative—depict what Saidiya Hartman calls the "abject sublime," the unfathomable horror of the transatlantic slave trade?[5] Various artworks seek to translate the experiences of those who lived under slavery, and most effective are firsthand accounts like those of Olaudah Equiano, Frederick Douglass, Harriet Jacobs, Solomon Northrup, or Zora Neale Hurston in her recently published *Barracoon,* in which she records the testimony of Kudjo Lewis, one of the last slaves brought over from Africa to the United States. The impossible choices of the enslaved person—losing one family member, or leaving behind another, for instance—can be depicted visually, narratively, or, here, ludically, but the place where the text breaks down, refusing the player's participation in the narrative, holds open an aporia that admits the broader impossibility of representation of the "abject sublime." In much the same way that the white space of a page can signal what cannot be

4. Stallabrass, "Just Gaming." On the issue of the slave's lack of agency, see Orlando Patterson, *Slavery and Social Death: A Comparative Study* (Cambridge, Mass.: Harvard University Press, 1982) and Vincent Brown's thoughtful address of the misuse of this abstraction, "Social Death and Political Life in the Study of Slavery," *American Historical Review* (December 2009), 1231–49.

5. Saidiya Hartman, "Response: The Dead Book Revisited," *History of the Present* 6, no. 2 (Fall 2016): 208–15.

captured in words or abstraction can stand in for the ineffable in the visual arts, these videogames use interruptions of immediacy to break the illusion of play.

By interrupting the player's complete absorption into the playable character's identity, such as by refusing a satisfying conclusion, these games highlight the impossibility of representing this history in an interactive form. Even if the player of *Following the Footsteps* successfully makes it to Philadelphia, the action doesn't conclude in a celebratory manner: "The first part of your journey is over. But the freedom of Canada is still days, weeks, even months away. Perhaps you'll never see it at all. But for now, you give thanks." The lack of a conclusion in *Footsteps* strands the player in Philadelphia, short of attaining freedom in Canada. We can compare this to the more decisive last words of the other online Underground narrative, "The Underground Railroad: Escape from Slavery," in which the "player" is situated more firmly as a spectator of Walter's narrative: "I don't know for sure what awaits me in Canada. But I do know this . . . I will not die a slave." Also of note is the iPad game's infinite loop, with the same ending offering the player another turn, no matter the outcome. Importantly, it does not feel possible to *win* these games.

I have elected not to include a thorough address of the aforementioned game *Freedom!* by MECC in this section, chiefly because its outdated technology makes it difficult for me to tell where the boundary between intentional limitations and my own frustration as a player with twenty-first-century expectations for graphics, gameplay, and maneuverability lies. Most simply put: I have had little success navigating the playable character more than a few millimeters across the map, and I feel incapable of determining whether this is due to a clever game design that highlights all of the various difficulties that a fugitive slave would encounter (as the "game over" screen boasts, when the player dies of snakebite, drowns, or is recaptured, for instance) or whether, frankly, I just suck at this game. But one final note: the designers of *Freedom!* made an odd choice.

If the playable character is literate, he or she can forge a pass and read signs along the way. If, however, the playable character is illiterate, the signs appear as indecipherable, squiggly lines. This would seem to be a strategy to heighten the player's immersion in the character. However, because these ciphers are shown on the same screen as all of the instructions and options from which the player must choose to advance the narrative, which are relayed to the player *in legible writing,* this visual depiction of illiteracy is an unconvincing and even ironic device that may only remind the player of his separation from the character. Nonetheless, I want to attend to where, in other games, such formal devices create definitive effects. We take our final example of a game aimed at elementary schoolchildren from *Mission US: Flight to Freedom.* In the spirit of Edmond Chang's method of "close-playing," I'll devote the next section to the analysis of this game's "intersection of form, function, meaning, and action."[6]

---

6. Edmond Chang, "Close Playing: A Meditation on Teaching with Videogames," *Edmond Chang* (website), November 11, 2010, http://www.edmondchang.com/2010/11/11/close-playing-a-meditation/.

A Close Playing: *Flight to Freedom*

FLIGHT TO FREEDOM is part of the series of educational games called *Mission US,* which includes titles about the American Revolution, immigrants at the turn of the twentieth century, and the Dust Bowl. In *Flight to Freedom,* the student plays the character of Lucy King, a fourteen-year-old on the King Plantation in Kentucky, who must make decisions about whether to follow orders or resist authority. Throughout the game, Lucy earns badges for building alliances, knowing when to play it safe, and for resistance and sabotage, such as when she directly disobeys orders. (Badges can also be earned for focusing on family, earning the trust of someone, or even relying on prayer in difficult times.) In five parts, plus a prologue and epilogue, the game guides the player through a series of tasks.

On the home screen, where the player can choose to start a new game or continue a previous one, we see our heroine in silhouette overlooking the horizon with the plantation set against the background of an old map. "Long John," an old chain gang work song recorded by Alan Lomax, whose lyrics tell of a man called "Long John" who runs off and is "long gone / like a turkey through the corn," plays in the background, foreshadowing Lucy's flight from the plantation.[1]

In the prologue, we hear Lucy's voice as she sets the scene of her daily life. We are told of the types of chores she must do, of the

1. Alan Lomax, ed., *Afro-American Spirituals, Work Songs, and Ballads* (Washington, D.C.: Library of Congress Archive of Folk Song, AFS L3). Sung by "Lightning" and a group of African American convicts at Darrington State Prison Farm, Sandy Point, Texas, 1934. Recorded by John A. and Alan Lomax.

mean overseer Mr. Otis, and of the various strategies that some slaves employ, like working slow, breaking things, or, alternatively, just trying to get along. In a poignant moment, Lucy tells the spectator—or "spect-actor," to use Brazilian dramatist Augusto Boal's term[2]—that her mother has warned her that having just turned fourteen, things will now become even more difficult for her. This may be an oblique reference to rape, but Lucy merely wonders how things can possibly get worse. At the end of the prologue, we see Lucy in the center of the frame, and the player is given instructions on how to play the game by collecting "Journey Badges" for the decisions made while playing *as* Lucy.

The game's perspective is fluid. Although the home screen and prologue show Lucy, the game most often operates in the first person POV: the viewer sees close-ups of the people with whom Lucy converses, as if looking through her eyes, with text boxes at the bottom of the screen where a response must be selected. Sites from around the plantation, such as the laundry trough where she must wash clothes, are displayed at an angle that suggests her viewpoint. Details like birds and field hands singing offscreen lend to the game's realism. Yet, at other points, we see Lucy in the frame in the third person perspective, sometimes with voice-over narration relaying her thoughts. And at other points, the narrative gives instructions using the second person pronoun "you" to address the player, putting him or her in Lucy's place. The game thus toggles between the first person, second person, and third person perspective. The player's ability to feel as if they embody Lucy's role is restricted by this continual shifting of perspective.

Hampering the player's control of Lucy, interactivity in the game is limited. In a few rare moments peppered throughout the game, Lucy is given a piece of information, but the player is only

2. This term has previously been applied to videogames in Holger Pötzsch, "Playing Games with Shklovsky, Brecht, and Boal: Ostranenie, V-Effect, and Spect-actors as Analytical Tools for Game Studies," *Game Studies* 17, no. 2 (December 2017), http://gamestudies.org/1702/articles/potzsch.

given one possible option to advance the narrative. This is first seen at the start of the game: "You wake up in your quarters. You hear your mother talking to another slave outside." Only a single option is given to the player, to click a box marked "Okay." This convention of highlighting the illusion of choice, wherein a button must be clicked but the player is only given one option, such as "Okay" or "Continue," is employed a few times throughout gameplay, foreshadowing one of the most interesting moments in the game, which occurs at the climax. Sometimes in the dialog box, too, only a single option is given for how to respond, but more often, the player has three or four choices from which to select.

The first chapter opens on a shot of the interior of a slave cabin as two voices are heard discussing the punishment of a slave called Henry, who was recently whipped. Henry expresses his desire to escape. The other voice belongs to Lucy's mother, and the player's first choice in the game is whether to continue eavesdropping on their conversation or go outside to join them. Here we learn (provided that certain options are selected to continue the conversation) that Henry has been falsely accused of destroying the "hemp break," a tool that he says was old and falling apart, and that he has been unfairly whipped for an act he didn't commit. This gives the player insight into the overseer's cruelty and the types of punishment that might be meted out to enslaved people.

In part one, Lucy navigates a day on the plantation, and she has options to commit acts of subterfuge and protect her fellows. The playable character (PC) is given a set of tasks, including both the chores she is given by the overseer, like feeding livestock and stocking the woodshed, and goals her mother gives her, including checking on her little brother in the yard and going to the creek to gather comfrey root to treat Henry's wounds from his recent flogging. She must do the latter without arousing the suspicions of the overseer. When he confronts her, the player has to select from dialogue choices at the bottom of the screen. This is a convention that will be repeated throughout the game as Lucy is accosted by various authority figures. She is often given a choice of staying silent, telling the truth, or lying, which is made clear to the player by the word "lie" in all caps and brackets prefacing the snippet of dialogue in the selection box. During this first level, which depicts Lucy's day on the plantation, she must traverse various dangers, including avoiding the ire of the overseer and being deferential to Ms. Sarah, the master's daughter, who clearly used to be Lucy's playmate but who now draws a stark distinction in their relationship as mistress and slave. At the same time, Lucy must perform acts of solidarity, such as gathering herbs to treat Henry's wounds, attending to the needs of her own family, advising her brother to continue his study of letters without getting caught, and passing information from the big house to those in the field.

Most fascinatingly, Lucy is given a choice between performing her tasks well and doing a shabby job, which illustrates that poor workmanship was one method of resistance employed by the enslaved, a fact that Lucy tells the player outright in the prologue. In these moments, the player must choose between options given, similar to how, when Lucy is engaged in dialogue, the player must select among a few possible responses. In these instances, however, the player selects Lucy's choice for how to proceed by clicking through a range of options, including taking one's time or rushing a task. My favorite moment from this first chapter occurs in Lucy's encounter with the passive-aggressive Ms. Sarah. Lucy can earn a persuasion badge for convincing Ms. Sarah to tell the overseer to let her out of her afternoon chores so that she can alter a dress for her, but she can also earn a resistance badge by purposefully tailoring the dress to be too low cut!

In comparison to the other games I've presented thus far, *Mission US: Flight to Freedom* provides a more nuanced portrait of the dangers of resistance. Being too obstinate on the plantation in the first level results in punishment with direct consequences that affect the subsequent gameplay. Talking back to the overseer seems to have the most direct effect, and I found that it was even possible to fail; if Mr. Otis is too angered by Lucy's retorts and slow working, she is sold South immediately, and the game ends.

Whether or not Lucy has played the opening chapter in a resistive manner, the PC is accused of purposefully setting the smokehouse on fire, and in part two she escapes in the company of Henry, the punished slave we met at the game's opening and a habitual runaway, who we find out over the course of part one is going to be sold at auction. As the pair make the journey northward to cross the Ohio River in the next chapter, options allow them to accumulate forged road passes and steal food from gardens. They must use connections on other plantations and the supportive channels of the Underground Railroad, making choices regarding where to hide and who can be trusted. The player must keep an eye on the food supply and find safe locations to rest to safeguard the characters' health.

The outcome here will differ depending on how the first level was played. On one playthrough, the overseer punishes Lucy's family by revoking a weekend pass to see her father on a neighboring plantation, which has an adverse effect later, when a pass allows Lucy to elude detection as she makes her escape. During this encounter, the player can show the pass given to her by her mother to three white men who accost the fleeing slaves. As they themselves are illiterate, the ruse works, and Lucy is free to continue the journey—unless, of course, the player back-sassed the overseer so much that her pass was revoked, in which case she will not have it in her satchel. The player is therefore made to feel the consequences of acts of resistance that are too direct, even as they are rewarded with the accumulation of badges for others.

When I first played *Flight to Freedom* several years ago, I took a day to get past the second level of this simple game—I got caught by the slave catchers or died of starvation and exposure every time I tried to escape until I was, at last, willing to abandon my traveling companion and accept a wagon ride north alone. I still haven't found a way for Henry and Lucy to remain together. On a subsequent playthrough, a forged pass obtained from Lucy's uncle at a neighboring plantation was detected by slavecatchers, and Lucy and Henry separated in fleeing them. I was able to get passage across the river by asking some men of color to hide me in their boat, stressing the important role that solidarity and cooperation played in slave resistance. The fact that Lucy and Henry must separate no matter how well the player navigates the escape challenge of part two demonstrates how the game sets insurmountable limits for the player. As these first two parts depict slavery and resistance in the most detail, I have focused on them, and I'll just sketch out more briefly the other chapters before drawing some conclusions on how the game's mechanics support its goals.

In part three, the player performs a series of tasks in Ohio, where Lucy is disguised as a relative of a free family of color that operates a laundry service. Although Lucy is purportedly free in Ohio, she still must evade recapture. Trying not to raise the suspicions of the many slavecatchers in the area is one of her objectives. She also becomes close to several people working on the cause of abolition and attempts to free her family members left behind on the King plantation. When picking up laundry from the local hotel, Lucy encounters a slavecatcher and accidentally comes away with an affidavit for the recapture of Henry. Discovering that he also has made it to Ohio, she can collaborate with abolitionists and free men to intercede when slavecatchers would attempt to recapture Henry and return him South. By picking up the affidavit along with the laundry, the player intervenes, ensuring that the slavecatchers are unable to make a legal arrest.

In part four, the player strengthens Lucy's connection to abolitionists and other freedom fighters who help to facilitate the escape of her brother, Jonah, who was left behind on the King Plantation. A brief interlude provides Jonah's narrative, as word is sent south to describe what action he should take, including garnering safe passage on a ship while dressed in the guise of a slave girl and accompanied by a white woman (presumably, one working with the Underground Railroad). But, Lucy's reunion with her brother is bittersweet, as it comes with the knowledge that their mother has been sold further south, to New Orleans, and out of the range of their network's allies.

In part five, the man posing as Lucy's uncle is illegally kidnapped (à la Solomon Northrup) by slavecatchers, and Lucy and Jonah help to gather evidence to free him in a court of law. They go to the site of his arrest to pick up the fragments of his free papers, which the corrupt slavecatchers have torn to shreds, and enlist white witnesses to testify that Morgan was a free man. This part of the quest works subtly to educate the player about the limits and corruption of the legal system: no women can be put forward as potential witnesses, the player is instructed that the opinions of black men will be worthless in court, and the testimony of known abolitionists will also bear less weight at trial. In this last chapter, we see how pivotal a role was played by the Fugitive Slave Act, as some white people are unwilling to testify and even to intervene when they see wrongdoing occurring for fear that they might be arrested.

This game has been criticized for packaging slavery as fodder for educational entertainment, but I would emphasize two points here.[3] First, following Lucy's quest, lessons are imparted to the player about prohibitions on slave literacy, the Fugitive Slave Act, and the abolitionist movement, which is actually treated with some nuance. For example, the twenty-third president of the United States Benjamin Harrison makes a brief appearance at an abolitionist meeting to discuss "colonization" as an option (meaning, returning blacks to Africa), and he presents his political position that slavery must be stopped from spreading further but not abolished completely. The player is invited to draw conclusions about the inadequacy of such positions, just as he or she is encouraged to find fault with the legal system depicted in part five.

Second, I would assert that the game only becomes *fun* if the player chooses the most subversive options available to Lucy. The first level, in which Lucy merely does her chores on the plantation, with the player having to continually click through a series

3. See, for example, Taylor Gordon, "Innovative or Insensitive?: Videogame Simulating US Slave Experience Leaves Educators Divided," *Atlanta Blackstar* (March 16, 2015), https://blerds.atlantablackstar.com/.

of tasks if she doesn't want to arouse the suspicions of the overseer, is fairly dull in its approximation of work. It's only when the
player chooses to steal eggs from the chicken coop, purposefully
work slowly and sabotage chores, including leaving the smokehouse unlocked for it to be pilfered, that the game becomes excit-
ing. Naturally, this brand of entertainment seems perverse, but the
game is not without educational merits as it presents the player
with difficult choices that will have in-game consequences.

At the end of part five, however, no matter how successful
Lucy was in facilitating a successful trial for her adoptive uncle
and encouraging others to flee to Canada, she is caught by a slavecatcher and sold at auction. This is the official end of the game,
although there is an epilogue in which the player's accumulated
badges determine the outcome of the sale and the character's future. Although the game officially ends on a tragic note, with Lucy
being sold, there are a range of positive outcomes that can be attained by playing the earned badges in the epilogue to construct a
conclusion for Lucy's story. In one version, Lucy is sold south and
lives out the rest of her days hoping to reunite with her mother.
In another, she is sold west and finds solace by starting a family with a man called Joseph. Some badges allow her to escape to
Canada and rejoin old friends. In one option, the player can use a
badge based on the relationship built with Henry and marry him
in Canada. Or, if the player has continued to learn to read throughout the quest, they can play the earned literacy badge to allow
Lucy to find employment as a white abolitionist's assistant and
eventually meet Frederick Douglass, Sojourner Truth, and Harriet
Beecher Stowe. A resistance badge, if attained by performing direct acts of subterfuge throughout the game, can be played to join
with Harriet Tubman and return to Maryland as a conductor on
the Underground Railroad. But despite the options available in the
epilogue, the game's official ending on the auction block performs
its most pivotal work.

As previously stated, the game's oscillation between the third,
second, and first person may interrupt the player's full absorption

in the narrative. As Lucy stands on the auction block, we plainly see her full figure, from a three-fourths angle, in the frame. Just before this, however, the player saw through her eyes as she was sitting with others, awaiting auction in a kind of pen or corral. The transition in this moment from the first person to third person as Lucy steps on to the auction block might serve to peel the player back to reality, to remind the child of his or her separation from the historical character of this fugitive slave. But the mechanics of the game had already begun to do this work before the perspective shift by defying expectations of how a game should work.

Whereas, for most of the game, the player is given choices to determine the course of action that Lucy will take, clicking from a pair or a set of options to designate a selection, such as "steal vegetables from a garden" or "go hungry," in this penultimate sequence where Lucy awaits her auction, only one button is provided, and clicking it merely brings up more text with the same button, which reads, "Okay." The same image is shown, from Lucy's point of view, of the other enslaved people waiting in the corral with her, as different descriptions appear in succession. For each new text block superimposed over the static image of a family embracing, the player has but one option: to click "Okay." This part of the narrative reads as such:

You are put into the pen where the slaves wait to be sold. [Okay]

There are guards everywhere. [Okay]

Across from you a woman sobs softly. [Okay]

Outside the auctioneer does his job. [Okay]

You never dreamed that you would be a slave again. [Okay]

As the player clicks the only available option, he or she hears the auctioneer splitting up a family. Despite the flatness of the animation, the game's architecture is profoundly affecting. While it may seem strange material for a game, or an odd medium in which to discuss a subject as serious as slavery, this educational instrument earns its badge as an interactive learning experience that handles the subject matter fairly delicately. However, somewhat ironically, this is achieved by the limits set on its own interactivity, especially in this moment, when it is mandated that the player click the only available option.

To my mind, the resistive potential of such "games" exists in moments like these, when they are less like *games* and more like an experience in line with the subject matter: when they exclude options, when they restrict the player's access, or—as in these frames where the player's only available option is to keep clicking "Okay"—when they give an illusion of choice that is not a choice at all. These are the moments when the game may seem to approximate the experience of slavery in digital form, but, more importantly, the game's mechanisms reinforce the separation of the player and the historical enslaved person, foreclosing the possibility that the historical slave can be occupied as an entertainment commodity.

In the next few sections, we will look at mainstream console videogames that aim at an older demographic and therefore incorporate more violent modes of resistance into the playable character's arsenal.

"Make History Yours": An Introduction to Assassin's Creed

THE HISTORY OF VIOLENT SLAVE REBELLION has sometimes become fodder for videogames. In 1988, a French company based in Bordeaux released an 8-bit computer game called *Freedom: Rebels in Darkness,* in which the player incarnates one of four playable enslaved characters on the Grand Parnasse plantation. After choosing to play as either Solitude, Makandal, Delia, or Sechou, the player navigates a maze-like layout on the main screen, being careful to avoid the dogs on patrol. At various points, the player may select a location on the map to bring up a further challenge screen, and there work to rally other slaves to the cause, burn down fields and storehouses, or else confront diverse enemies, at which point the game turns into a "street fighter" style game, depicting hand-to-hand combat. I have been unable to make significant progress in this game, but it certainly seems worthy of more investigation, especially given that historical figures like French clergyman, colonist, and slave owner Pere Labat (1663–1738) and one of the most famous rebel slaves of all time, François Makandal (executed 1758), are alluded to in the game.

Despite the outdated technology, *Rebels in Darkness* can be accessed in an English language version on Dosbox via the Internet Archive. Various restrictions hamper progress, and as such, the vintage game foreshadows some of the tools that more recent games have purposefully employed to safeguard the subject of the historical rebel enslaved person. *Rebels in Darkness* begins by asking the player for a passcode that was included in the box to eliminate piracy, but the patient player can merely keep guessing from the provided answers until they turn up the right one.

After this, the scene is set with the following description:

> Night is falling over the prosperous Grand Parnasse plantation. The slaves, under their supervisor's thumb, have left the carts of cane and gone back to their huts. Meanwhile, the owner sips his rum on the veranda and the director rubs his hands; the plantation makes a considerable profit. The accountant finishes his records; there are 200 casks of sugar piled up in the buildings. The supervisor is worried. The lashes of his whip are no longer enough to keep the rhythm in the fields. The wind of rebellion is blowing over the negroes' huts! But who would dare become the leader of a rebellion?

Some of the odd word choice here ("director," "supervisor") may be due to translation; doubtless, a native English speaker would say "overseer" in place of "supervisor." However, Martinican author Patrick Chamoiseau is credited with writing the text of the game, and it seems appropriately subversive: the player can burn down the storehouse, with the two hundred casks of sugar inside, effectively destroying the master's profits. But without the full instructions, many aspects of the game remain mysterious, from which buttons will have an effect to more complex matters. Most importantly, for our immediate purposes, the game exists as a relic of a bygone era, which limits its accessibility and makes it rather difficult to play. Due to modern expectations for gameplay and quality of graphics, *Rebels in Darkness* offers little immersion for the 2020 player.

In 2009, a Brazilian company called Donsoft Entertainment produced a game called *Capoeira Legends: Paths to Freedom,* which depicts the nation's proud history of slave resistance. The game focuses on the Maroons, fugitive slaves who formed their own communities and purportedly used martial arts to fight the Portuguese colonizers. Set in 1828, near Rio de Janeiro, the game depicts the use of capoeira against "advocates of slavery" by those who would preserve their freedom.[1] Gameplay appears to mainly in-

---

1. For more on videogames from Brazil, see Lynn Rosalina Gama Alves, "Brazil," in *Video Games around the World,* edited by Mark J. Wolf (Cambridge, Mass.: MIT Press, 2015), 88.

volve combat against the uniformed militia and colonizer civilians who would subdue the playable character, Gunga Za. However, a full treatment of this game would necessitate a nuanced depiction of cultural attitudes about slavery in Brazil, and my rudimentary command of Brazilian Portuguese prohibits me, at this point, from attempting a more in-depth study. Nonetheless, both *Rebels in Darkness* and *Capoeira Legends* provide a good introduction to the more detailed discussion of other games that follows here: games where physical violence against slavers, slaveholders, and planta-tion masters becomes a part of the play. In the next few sections, we will see how passcodes, language barriers, and moments that obstruct player immersion create a pause in which we ought to re-flect on commodification and co-option of the identity of the rebel slave in the game.

In recent years, the videogame company Ubisoft has created two games within the Assassin's Creed series that make freeing the enslaved a major component of the gameplay. A trademark of the franchise is the facilitation of missions within historical time periods of interest, like the American and French Revolutions. The games in the series aspire to historical accuracy, most in-clude multiple languages, and they are all prefaced with this note: "Inspired by historical events and characters, this work of fiction was designed, developed and produced by a multicultural team of various religions, faiths and beliefs." The historical accura-cy of the backdrops is obviously important to Ubisoft, and game scholar Adrienne Shaw has addressed their successes and short-comings on this score in her address of *Assassin's Creed III*, about the American Revolution. Shaw illustrates how the game works against itself (and the critique it works hard to demonstrate itself making) and instead ends up foreclosing any real emancipatory potential.[2] This assessment also rings true of the games I'm look-

2. In an important article, Adrienne Shaw discusses problems in the series's retelling of the American Revolution and the narrative limits of the game's critique of history. See Adrienne Shaw, "The Tyranny of Realism:

ing at here, wherein the series' intervention in the history of slave rebellion is both productive and destructive to our understanding of that resistance and its legacy. In my discussion of Assassin's Creed, I'll focus on two games, both part of the Americas series of the universe, the stand-alone game *Liberation,* and *Freedom Cry,* downloadable content (DLC) for *Assassin's Creed IV Black Flag,* about pirates in the Caribbean. These games are not central parts of the hero's quest, but ancillary narratives—*Liberation* was first released in 2012 for the handheld gaming device the PS Vita and only made available for the main consoles in 2014, and *Freedom Cry* was only ever accessible as a supplementary DLC—indicating the lower priority of these characters' tales as compared to the major releases of the central series titles.

Liberation opens in French New Orleans one hundred years before the American Civil War. In the game, the player incarnates a free woman of color, Aveline de Grandpré, who is the daughter of a slave from Saint Domingue and her white master. Aveline's mother disappeared when she was just a child, and she was raised by her white father and stepmother, wealthy merchants. The game begins with the playable character reliving a memory of childhood loss, in which the young Aveline sees slaves being auctioned on the block and then traumatically loses her mother in the marketplace. This cut-scene has been a dream and Aveline awakens to find herself in the year 1763, in which she is a young lady, raised in elegant society, but is dividing her time as an Assassin.

Liberation's gameplay includes a series of missions, some of which are concerned with the treatment of slaves and in which Aveline aids in their escape to the Bayou or investigates their disappearance and displacement to the colony of Chichen Itza in Mexico, but most of which are about battles for control of territory among corrupt colonial governors and intrigue among smugglers

Historical Accuracy and Politics of Representation in *Assassin's Creed III,*" *Loading. . . . The Journal of the Canadian Game Studies Association* 9, no. 14 (2015): 4–24.

in the swamplands. The theme of liberating the slaves is present here, though it seems subsidiary to Aveline's efforts to uncover the truth about her mother's involvement with the Assassin syndicate and even her efforts to help her father's business. In one mission, for example, she buys out a competitor to pay his slaves a living wage, thereby liberating them via capitalism. In short, despite Aveline's goals, stated at one point when she is speaking to her mentor, Agaté, as being to "free the slaves, defeat our enemies, impose justice," for most of the game there is an absence of a radical abolitionist message.

I echo here Shaw's disappointment in her analysis of *Assassin's Creed III,* for although *Liberation* espouses a revolutionary ethic— as when Aveline delivers lines like "Anyone who keeps slaves deserves to lose them"—the game seemingly fails to deliver on these words. Aveline continues managing her father's shipping routes for trade in commodities like cotton and tobacco, sending ships to Cuba and Veracruz in exchange for money, but she is still working within a society (and therefore affecting supply and demand) that exploits slave labor. In fact, it isn't made clear until late in the game that Aveline is aware of and frustrated by her relative powerlessness to change society. Ultimately, *Liberation* fails to live up to its name.

Whereas Haiti and its legacy of slave revolt is a backdrop in *Liberation,* as Aveline's mother and her mentor Agaté are both from Saint Domingue, the French colony that would wage a war for its independence to become the first black republic, Saint Domingue is the primary setting of *Freedom Cry.* In this DLC, the player incarnates a character called Adewalé, a former slave and quartermaster to Edward Kenway, the central playable character in the pirate adventure *Assassin's Creed IV Black Flag.* In *Freedom Cry,* the player incarnates Adewalé as he journeys to Saint Domingue, frees slaves, and falls in league with a band of Maroons waging a war against the colonial governor.

The basic plot of the narrative is relatively simple: after taking hold of a package during a battle with a Templar fleet, Adewalé shipwrecks just off the island of Saint Domingue. Adewalé's first challenge comes when he stumbles upon a white overseer about to attack a female slave. The overseer hisses threats (spoken only in French) that he will cut off her ears if she doesn't submit. Grabbing hold of the first weapon he sees, a machete, what was historically the tool of the cane-cutting slave, Adewalé chases down the overseer. This is the player's first objective on the island, which lends us our title: "Kill the Overseer." After the player, incarnating Adewalé, slays the would-be assailant and receives thanks from the victim, he begins his new role as a liberator of the enslaved.

Because he successfully absconded with the Templar's parcel, addressed to one Bastienne Josephe in Port-au-Prince, he goes to find her. She is a wealthy and influential madam with connections to both the leader of the Maroon renegades and the colonial governor, which, in addition to her presumed connection to the Templars, causes Adewalé to distrust her, and he withholds the package. The feeling is mutual, and she gives him a series of tasks to prove himself. Through her, Adewalé connects with Augustin Dieufort, the leader of the Maroons, and performs several missions in which he frees slaves, kills white jailors, and unlocks the enchained. He eventually takes on other missions through his alliances with Augustin Dieufort and Bastienne Josephe. Even more pronouncedly than the game called *Liberation,* this game makes the liberation of slaves the player's chief *labor* in the game. Recruiting Maroons along the way, Adewalé liberates plantations and slave ships, ultimately winning a ship for the cause and teaching Augustin to man it for the coming "revolution"—the objective of which is stated as "Maroon independence." Adewalé also performs tasks for Bastienne, mainly providing intel, for example by spying on the harbormaster and gleaning information about a scientific expedition in which the Gouvernor de Fayet has invested.

If Shaw is concerned with the identity politics involved in making a Native character playable in *Assassin's Creed III,* we should also question the playable character of the rebel slave in games like *Liberation* and *Freedom Cry.* To fully treat this subject, one would have to undertake a sociological study of the players' investment in the game and their feelings regarding the stakes of inhabiting Aveline and Adewalé. Taking such an approach would necessitate a transnational perspective with the participation of gamers and game designers from countries like Brazil and Martinique, who might have a different perspective on the appropriateness of making historical slave resistance a playable quest. But to look at it another way, concentrating only on formal construction, we find that such games often highlight the difficulty of representation of this history in an interactive mode. One way that the Assassin's Creed franchise addresses this issue, what we might think of as "avatar trouble," is by drawing attention to the playability of the character, effectively metagaming the discomfort of making the historical rebel slave a playable character.[3]

The world of Assassin's Creed spans many centuries and is a large playground, but by means of a fantastical frame, the playable characters' lives are packaged as an entertainment experience for others. Besides the purported realism of the in-game play, and in direct contrast to the aspirational historical fidelity of the series, there's a whole element to the Assassin's Creed franchise of secret societies, time travel, and an alien race. Although this is not my primary concern here, suffice it to say that the central intrigue concerns a long-standing war between the Brotherhood of the Assassins and the secretive order of the Templars, who wage their battles throughout history by the means of a device called the Animus, which allows characters to access their ancestors' memories and, in a virtual sense, be transported back in time. Within most of the Assassin's Creed games, then, the player is *playing*

3. Here I use the word "metagaming" in a manner that is in line with Andy Baio, "Metagames: Games about Games," Waxy, February 1, 2011, https://waxy.org/2011/02/metagames_games_about_games/. But see Stephanie Boluk and Patrick Lemieux, *Metagaming: Playing, Competing, Spectating, Cheating, Trading, Making, and Breaking Videogames* (Minneapolis: University of Minnesota Press, 2017) for a complete discussion of all that this term can encompass.

at being rather than merely *playing as* the characters that live in recognizably historical settings. The layered nature of the player's occupation of the playable character highlights the occupation of others' bodies as a central problem of the gameplay.

The fictional corporation Abstergo Industries is a front for the Templars, and the Animus device allows the game's characters to inhabit people who lived in the past. In most of the games in the Assassin's Creed universe, the player incarnates Desmond Miles, a presumably white male living in the future in a frame narrative. Miles uses the Animus machine to channel the historical figures he animates, like Connor, his Mohawk ancestor in *Assassin's Creed III,* set during the American Revolution. The issue of how much these characters' playability should bother us seems to pivot on the question of audience. If we imagine, as Shaw does, the intended audience to be the same demographic that Miles represents (white men), then the incarnation of bodies of color and their historical struggles may be read as problematic, but it is important to note that scholars are divided on this issue. As Kishonna Grey and Jordan Mazurek note, "gamers of color frequently use and reference [imagery from games such as these] as one of personal empowerment."[4] Regardless, the fictional Abstergo Industries' motto, "Make history yours," concedes both the potential payoff and pitfall of these games. As Shaw has noted, in the Assassin's Creed series, history is commoditized, and this is particularly fraught when the legacy of resistance—whether that of the indigenous or the enslaved—is being offered up for occupation and reclamation, digitally commodified as interactive adventures.

The two Assassin's Creed games I'm concerned with here, *Liberation* and *Freedom Cry,* avoid some of Shaw's concerns, as they cast off the frame narrative of Desmond Miles, and therefore,

4. Kishonna Grey and Jordan Mazurek, "Visualizing Blackness—Racializing Gaming: Social Inequalities in Virtual Gaming Communities," in *The Routledge International Handbook of Visual Criminology,* edited by Michelle Brown and Eamonn Carrabine (New York: Routledge, 2017), 18.

the player is not hailed into the position of a white man occupying the lives of people of color. And yet, these games offer a more direct co-option of the histories of black resistance, which we might interpret as even more problematic. Miles standing as an intermediary between the player and the historical character establishes an additional layer of distance between the player and the playable character that is lacking in these games. But both *Liberation* and *Freedom Cry* excise the frame narrative of Desmond Miles. I've heard two scholars, Amanda Philips and Soraya Murray, note in recent talks that *Liberation* is the first game of the series in which Abstergo Industries, the fictional company that controls the Animus device, offers its services to the general public, allowing an unnamed subject (most immediately, the player) to experience the memories of a supposedly historical person directly.[5] That is, in *Liberation*'s frame narrative, Aveline is *for sale*. Her story is not just available to her ancestors (as with the Desmond Miles games) but to anyone who will pay to play. It is indeed notable that the first black protagonist depicted in the franchise, a "freedom fighter" (in Soraya Murray's words) and a product of slavery herself, is offered up as a commodity. Because of the game's fictional frame as content produced by Abstergo for consumption, there is a sense that the player is piloting Aveline directly.

Similarly, Miles's frame is absent in *Freedom Cry*. In brief, though we are given a bit of the backstory of the former slave turned assassin in the game trailer and in *Black Flag* (where we are introduced to Adewalé as a non-playable character), in the DLC in which he is the central protagonist, the narrative of his previous life is mostly absent. We know he is a former slave from a

5. Here I am referring to Soraya Murray, "The Visual Poetics of Video Games" (talk, Texas Tech University, Lubbock, Tex., February 16, 2016, http://www.depts.ttu.edu/ART/SOA/nav/landmark/speakerschedule.php) and Amanda Phillips, "Nothing Is True: Racial Hybridity, Manipulated Memory, and White Innocence in *Assassin's Creed III*" (paper, Society for Cinema and Media Studies Annual Conference 2016, Atlanta, Ga.).

sugarcane plantation in Trinidad and that he sailed with Edward Kenway aboard the *Jackdaw* in *Black Flag*. In *Freedom Cry*, however, Adewalé finds new purpose beyond pirating, and the player is dropped directly into his life without the frame of a player incarnating him via the Animus.

In examining Aveline and Adewalé as our playable protagonists, then, there are several strands that must be separated. Without the frame of Desmond Miles acting as a bulwark against the full absorption of the player into the role of the playable character, we might feel that the occupation of the historical subject position of the rebel slave is more immediately offered to the player. However, as with the other games included in this study, I'll argue here that the games' elisions productively foreclose complete occupation of the playable characters in other ways. One of the ways this is achieved is by underlining the games *as fictions*.

Avatar Trouble and Aveline

MORE THAN JUST MOVING BODIES across a digital landscape, many videogames exhibit the "second person conundrum" described by Jill Walker in her essay "Do You Think You're Part of This?: Digital Texts and the Second Person Address." Walker writes, "In many digital texts, identification is pushed as far as possible . . . the difference between *playing* and *being* is blurred."[1] In a similar manner, in many games depicting slave resistance, the player is invited to identify with, to control, to *become* a slave-in-revolt in some capacities and explicitly denied that position in others. This use of the second person is exhibited, for example, in the directive mentioned above, from *Freedom Cry*: "Kill the overseer!"

"Kill the overseer!" is not a suggestion, or a piece of advice—it's a command. If you don't kill the overseer, you fail. You are "desynchronized" from the gameplay and must begin again. If you want the game to progress, you have no choice but to chase after the overseer, who in this instance is in pursuit of the female slave whose ears he threatens to cut off. When you catch him, you dispatch him on the spot with the machete and the game allows you to advance. Similar injunctions are seen in other videogames that feature slave revolt, like "Incite a riot" or "Fight the slave-masters" (both from *Assassin's Creed Liberation*), and I'm interested here in how the traditional form of interactive games, with a set of directives that must be followed, takes on a deeper resonance when the subject at hand is historical enslavement and rebellion.

1. Jill Walker, "Do You Think You're Part of This?: Digital Texts and the Second Person Address," *CyberText Yearbook 2000,* edited by Markku Eskelinen and Raine Koskimaa (Saarijärvi, Finland: Gummerus Printing, 2001), 44.

Game designer Sid Meier said that all games are "a series of interesting choices," but it doesn't always feel this way. As with the command "Kill the overseer," some directives are not *choices* in a certain type of adventure game. Without completing the task at hand, the player does not advance the journey or narrative. Citing Meier's famous line, Ian Bogost writes in *Persuasive Games,* "Interesting choices do not necessarily entail all possible choices in a given situation; rather, choices are selectively included and excluded in a procedural representation to produce a desired and expressive end."[2] That is, as we've seen in our discussion of *Mission US: Flight to Freedom,* it is not always *choice* that enhances the play; sometimes, it is the lack of it. Most interesting are those moments when games about rebel slaves work subversively by *not working:* when options are disenabled, when the game seems to glitch, when the player is reminded of his or her separation from the protagonist. The game seems to subtly say, "Kill the overseer, but remember, as you're doing it, that this is only a game, and that *you* are not the historical person you are controlling."[3] Without the frame narrative of Desmond Miles lending to the game a Russian Doll effect, whereby the player incarnates a character incarnating another character, *Liberation* and *Freedom Cry* may seem to efface the distance between the player and the playable character, but other devices hold open that space.

A player's identification with the avatar can be affected both by perspective and maneuverability. Neither of the Assassin's Creed games I'm discussing here is in the first person perspective, as are many of the Underground Railroad games presented in the early

2. Bogost, *Persuasive Games,* 45.
3. In this way, the games I'm looking at here seem to function like others that draw attention to themselves as games. For an example of this, see James Sweeting, "Illusions of Choice in Digital Narratives" in *Transtechnology Research Reader 2015–2017* (Plymouth, U.K.: University of Plymouth, 2018), in which he discusses the game *Spec Ops: The Line* and its strategy of embracing "ludonarrative dissonance" to encourage players to reflect upon their role in playing violent military videogames.

sections of this volume—*Mission US,* for example. But nor is it in a distant third person perspective, as in *Thralled,* a game I'll discuss later, in which the playable character's body is always seen, in profile, on the screen of the two-dimensional platform game. In *Liberation* and *Freedom Cry,* as in all of the Assassin's Creed games, the perspective is set slightly above and behind the protagonist's body so that most of the in-game action feels like a follow shot, with the player capable of manipulating the perspective with a rotating "camera." Except for the cinematic cut-scenes, during which the player has no control over the characters on screen, the player wields control of the PC's body, pressing buttons to advance, to run, to shoot, to throw a punch, and even, in the case of *Liberation*'s Aveline, to flirt as a subversive strategy. Yet, beyond the game's mechanics, both Assassin's Creed games use narrative to underline the issue of identity, subterfuge, and playing at being someone else.

Importantly, identity is a central feature of the narrative in *Liberation.* Aveline has three costumes that she wears throughout the game, each coming with different skill sets and eliciting different treatment by the community as she walks through the city in the assassin's garb, the slave's rags, or the lady's gown. Aveline's outfits, which have varied abilities, are given to the player at the start, but others can be bought with in-game currency or by accumulating certain objects in the gameplay. This aspect underscores what Stallabrass says about the role of the commodity in videogames: "Games obsequiously reflect the operation of consumer capital for they are based on exchange, an incessant trading of money, munitions or energy, a shuttling back and forth of goods and blows." However, this takes on new importance in a game about the commodification of humans.[4]

In her discussion of the game, Murray attends to the fact that Aveline's prowess and maneuverability change depending on which

4. Stallabrass, "Just Gaming."

persona she dons.[5] As Murray has suggested, we might make much of the diversity of this avatar and her ability to maneuver through society in a variety of roles. Aveline's malleability stresses the different levels of social freedom offered to whites and to free people of color in the historical setting. Indeed, the fact that pressing the same buttons on the controller will have different effects depending on whether your avatar is wearing the costume of the slave, the assassin, or the lady undergirds the themes of slavery and freedom in the haptics of the game. Sometimes, forgetting which guise I had adopted, I would frustratingly mash the button to scale a fence or climb a roof and find it had no effect because I was in the lady's form. I'd then have to locate one of the many changing stations in the town before I could switch costumes. Somewhat ironically, physical mobility in this sense (not being able to climb or even run outright) is limited when Aveline represents the wealthy free woman of color, though it is true that wearing other guises, like the assassin's outfit, comes with its own limitations, such as being more vulnerable to detection. The convention of having different outfits change the player's abilities is in no way unique to this game, but it takes on important significatory work given the game's narrative. Murray discusses the persona system alongside its "poetics of form" in a compelling way, arguing that social mobility and racial "passing" are literalized in the mechanics of this game. But one aspect we might look at (beyond Aveline's differing abilities depending upon her outfits, which alternately provide talent in diplomacy, blending in, or combat strength) is how her changing appearance elicits varied responses from the passersby, revealing how she is perceived in the community and stressing that all three types of black bodies— free woman of color, the slave, and the rebel slave—are rendered as spectacles that play distinctly to diverse stereotypes.

The lady persona often draws lascivious comments from men of low social standing such as the sailors and dockworkers. Examples

5. Murray, "Visual Poetics."

include "Care for a dance, miss?" and "Am I not handsome enough for you?" At one point, Aveline interrogates the drunk captain of a ship, who jokes that in his inebriated state he sees three of her (a nod to her triple persona) but makes it clear that he is up to the challenge of satisfying all three sexually. Doubtless, a scholar like Kimberly Manganelli, who has written on the quadroon society of New Orleans and the "Tragic Mulatta," would have much to say about the sexualization of this mixed race character and of the game's portrait of mixed race society in New Orleans.[6] One of the most problematic aspects of the game, to my mind, is the fact that Aveline's beauty is considered a weapon. When she wears the guise of the lady, she is capable of "charming" enemies out of information and jewelry. She can shoot them with a poison blow dart that comes out of her parasol, but she can't even climb a fence in her paniers. *Liberation*'s rich diversity of experience regarding a single character avatar wearing different outfits signals to the issue of participatory spectatorship, which mirrors the way that a player can don a digital guise that may be different from his or her own in terms of class, race, gender, and, certainly, time period.

Aveline's changing appearance also therefore acts as a kind of meta-commentary on the game itself, where the player takes on an identity that doesn't properly belong to him or her. Just as this wealthy, free woman of color pretends to be a slave in order to aid her campaign, so too, is the contemporary gamer donning a digital costume and playing at a role within the historical context of slave resistance. Such "metagaming" moments (here I mean the word in the sense of *meta*fictional, self-referential nods to the medium itself) are prevalent throughout videogames, and they may work to interrupt the player's absorption in the drama, underlining the

6. Kimberly Manganelli, *Transatlantic Spectacles of Race: The Tragic Mulatta and the Tragic Muse* (New Brunswick, N.J.: Rutgers University Press, 2012). See also Emily Clark, *The Strange History of the American Quadroon: Free Women of Color in the Revolutionary Atlantic World* (Chapel Hill: University of North Carolina Press, 2015).

fiction of the play. Centrally, in interactive narratives about slavery, they work to emphasize the player's separation from the real historical lives from which the game draws.[7] Similar to what we encounter in *Liberation,* Adewalé's abilities in the game *Freedom Cry* are also dramatically decreased in one mission when he is dressed in the slave's garb. Effecting a kind of "operationalized weakness" in which player characters have purposefully limited abilities, such moments can frustrate the player in a productive manner that also serves to highlight the fiction of the game, but we will turn to this topic in a later section.[8] There's one final point I want to make on the "avatar trouble" highlighted by the game *Liberation.*

Besides the diversity of experiences Aveline's triple persona offers the player, there may also be an acknowledgment of the inherently plural nature of history, as is also present within the game's emphasis on secret histories and uncovered truths. We might read this as a way the game safeguards itself from accusations of historical trespass, or, more generously, we could argue it preserves a space for considering the inaccessible history of day-to-day slave resistance, one unlikely to have been recorded in the plantation logs or masters' journals, which unfortunately form the basis of much of our understanding of the lives of the enslaved. This gap in our record is encapsulated in a phrase graffitied on the wall of the Elmina slave fort in Ghana: "Until the lion has his historian, the hunter will always be a hero."[9] But unfortunately, this potentially pluralist view of history is one of the places where I would say that *Liberation* fails to live up to its liberatory promise.

There is a subplot in *Liberation* in which a hacker called Erudito contacts the player at various points in the game and offers re-

7. See Boluk and Lemieux, *Metagaming;* their own use of the term "metagame" is broad, including games about games, games within games, and the worlds around games, to articulate a kind of ecology of play.

8. For a discussion of operationalized weakness, see Bogost, *How to Do,* 20. For a discussion on the uses of frustration in videogames, see Gilleade and Dix, "Using Frustration."

9. A photograph is displayed at SlaveHaven Museum in Memphis.

vealing glimpses into how Abstergo Industries has tampered with
or redacted Aveline's storyline. This further distances the player
and the playable character, as the player is addressed directly and
thereby separated from the role he or she is playing as Aveline. In
these moments, an electronic voice-over tells the player to find a
character called "Citizen E" and assassinate him. If this is accom-
plished, the player revisits a previously seen cut-scene, this time
with modifications or extra lines that reveal "the truth" Abstergo has
presumably hidden. For example, the third reveal replays a conversation between Gérald Blanc (Aveline's business associate, would-be
suitor, and sometime accomplice) and Aveline (in slave costume) in
which she expresses dissatisfaction that she cannot do more for the
enslaved. Aveline says, "A small gesture, hardly enough. I can offer
them a wage, but what good is money without freedom?" Here she
acknowledges that her personal efforts in paying her own workers
rather than keeping them enslaved does not undo the problems of
the society at large. She also expresses feelings of powerlessness
going up against the Templars, who will "never allow the slaves to
be free." Perhaps it is only these references to the Templars that are
meant to be redacted, but nonetheless Erudito's recoveries reveal
more subversive content, expressing a greater scope to Aveline's
goals for the emancipation of the enslaved.

By definition, cut-scenes interrupt the player's sense of control over the PC, as the gameplay is suspended while the player
becomes an inactive spectator witnessing a cinematic interlude.
But in Erudito's reveals, in which we revisit previously seen material with new content disclosed, the PC is doubled via déjà vu,
establishing a further distance between the player and the character of Aveline and destabilizing player impressions of the game.
Erudito's final "hack" comes after the credits roll at the conclusion of the game, revealing an alternate ending in which Aveline
takes an oath of loyalty to the Brotherhood, administered by her
stepmother Madeleine. This scene uncovers that Madeleine had
been the adversary Aveline was tracking all along, dubbed "The
Company Man," and that it was, in fact, Madeleine who killed

Aveline's father, who purportedly dies of illness midway through the game. After slaying her evil stepmother, Aveline completes the "Prophesy Disk" (a much-coveted object in the game, shards of which Aveline had collected in missions on Chichen Itza) with her locket, an heirloom from her mother. This action reveals a holo-gram about a character called "Eve" who will lead the people to freedom. It is intimated that Aveline (meaning "little Eve") will go on to bring about real emancipation for the slaves. But even as this game would package itself as progressive, and Erudito's hacks of-ten reveal a more revolutionary narrative, the game's construction of its own alternative history is not without complications.

As I've discussed elsewhere in more detail, several historical flashpoints of slave resistance in the colony of Saint Domingue are woven into the plots of both *Liberation* and *Freedom Cry*.[10] The commoditization of the history of slave resistance in the only colony where enslaved peoples successfully led a rebellion that established a sovereign nation reeks of an incorporation and anes-thetization of Haiti's history in the form of an entertainment com-modity. Most troublingly, the game incorporates into its fiction the historical personage of François Makandal, Maroon leader of Saint Domingue, whose efforts at poisoning the white slaveholding community some historians consider to be the first chapter of the Haitian Revolution.[11] This is starkly different from the subtle nod to the historic Makandal in the game *Freedom: Rebels in Darkness*. A complete account of how Makandal is referenced in *Liberation* is beyond our scope here, but in short, the narrative implies that

10. Sarah Juliet Lauro, "Digital Saint-Domingue: Playing Haiti in Videogames," *sx archipelagos* 2 (September 2017), http://smallaxe.net /sxarchipelagos/issue02/playing-haiti.html.

11. Laurent Dubois describes Makandal as an important precursor to the Haitian Revolution. Laurent Dubois, *Avengers of the New World: The Story of the Haitian Revolution* (Cambridge, Mass.: Harvard University Press, 2004). See also Carolyn Fick, *The Making of Haiti: The Saint Domingue Revolution from Below* (Knoxville: University of Tennessee Press, 1990).

the historic rebel slave François Makandal was a member of the fictional Brotherhood of Assassins in a move that is a dangerous co-option of black resistance by the entertainment industry.

In the game, Aveline battles a bayou witchdoctor calling himself François Mackandal, who is in league with the corrupt Spanish official de Ferrer seeking control of the colony. The False Mackandal, as he is called in the game—it is later revealed that his name is actually Baptiste—was formerly acquainted with both Aveline's mentor, Agaté, and her mother, Jeanne. Aveline comes to understand the False Mackandal's true identity and his relationship as protégé to the "real" Makandal. Importantly, the historical Makandal is referenced but never depicted in the game. The player can finish the game and attain "full synchronization" without learning much more about Makandal. However, if the player decides to collect the thirty pages of Jeanne's diary that are scattered throughout New Orleans and reveals the "hacks" hidden in the game by Erudito, a more complete and destructive picture emerges: one in which Aveline's mother obstructed Makandal's plan to poison the white slaveholding population of Saint Domingue, an actual event that led to the man's execution in the year 1758. Makandal's revolutionary command is gelded by his mere incorporation into this game, and his legacy is sublimated. In the game, Makandal is thwarted by Jeanne, our protagonist's mother, and his brand of emancipation is demonized. The "lord of poison" is depicted explicitly as a *failure* who died without succeeding at his mission. As many note, revision of history is endemic to the Assassin's Creed series, but I feel that these tamperings in history take on dangerous resonances when it is a legacy of slave resistance that is nerfed.[12]

Historical people are often referenced in the Assassin's Creed series. I disapprove of the treatment of Makandal in this game,

12. In addition to Shaw, see also James Patton, "Colonising History: The Culture and Politics of *Assassin's Creed*," *James Patton* (website), November 29, 2014, https://james-patton.net/2014/11/29/colonising-history-the-culture-and-politics-of-assassins-creed/.

and I would argue that the stakes are high when the game allows a player to incarnate the historical slave and the historical slave-in-revolt. But a more generous reading might assert that, in part, *Liberation* seems to acknowledge this. By doubling Makandal, and creating a character called "the False Mackandal," the game may point to itself as tampering with history and thus acknowledge itself as fiction. But for the player who neglects to do outside research, taking the game's representation of Makandal at face value, any reading of the symbolism of Makandal's doubling in "the False Mackandal" will surely be illegible. In the next section, we delve deeper into the issue of whether some moments of illegibility and player obstruction in the Assassin's Creed series can be read as charged with productive potential because of how they separate the player from the role she would inhabit in the game.

Untranslated

LIKE MANY GAMES in the Assassin's Creed franchise, both *Liberation* and *Freedom Cry* include snatches of untranslated language. Foreign languages (that is, languages that differ from the player's designated settings) are typically only translated in brackets within the cut-scenes *and* only if the player has enabled subtitles, which act like closed captioning. Subtitles provide text for all spoken dialogue in these scripted cinematic interludes and put translations in brackets when that speech has been delivered in a language other than the player's preferred one.[1] However, foreign languages heard in the gameplay are never translated for the player, and I'm arguing here that this linguistic gulf provides a productive obstacle to the player's complete absorption into the playable character's identity.

To fully understand how the community views Aveline, for example, the player needs to understand what the townspeople say to her (and about her) as she passes by. This is something that might be overlooked by most U.S. players, as the majority of these comments are untranslated and in French. If Aveline bumps into a stranger while wearing the lady's gown, she is treated politely: "Pardonnez-moi, mademoiselle." There is a polite inflection in the women's voices and, sometimes, a slightly lustful one in the men's.

---

1. This is another hallmark of the franchise. For example, in *Assassin's Creed III*, in addition to the use of the Mohawk language for which the game is famous, there are bits of French, German, Russian, and Portuguese. For a sense of how the gamer community views the AC series language options and the lack thereof, see Dustin Bailey, "*Assassin's Creed Odyssey* won't let you play in Greek," PCGamesN, August 13, 2018, https://www.pcgamesn.com/assassins-creed-odyssey/assassins-creed-odyssey-greek-language.

Yet, when this same lady finds herself in a different part of town (near the cemetery, where there are more people of color, for instance), a black woman says as she passes: "Look at her, making herself out to be a lady." The game therefore provides a rich diversity of experience, even across the treatment of the single character avatar, but this might be lost on the non-francophone player.

To analyze this element of the game, I performed an experiment in which I stood on a bustling corner in the game's setting of colonial New Orleans, or, more properly, Nouvelle Orléans, and relentlessly bumped into the townspeople. I performed this same action wearing each of the three costumes. I noted the gendered nature of the responses, looking for differences depending on time of day or location, and indeed there are many. I couldn't get slaves or people of color to respond to my affronts ever when in the guise of the lady or the assassin in the town square, but when dressed as a slave, and in any area where there were more people of color than whites, I could garner an "Attention!" or a "Je te connais?" [Do I know you?]. In the city square, the well-dressed people of color might audibly grunt, but they don't verbalize their objections. Yet the assassin can provoke a response such as "vous êtes pas bien" [roughly, you ain't right] when in a less prosperous part of town, but she is still addressed with the formal "vous." Similarly, while the white *citoyens* respond to the lady with the utmost politesse, it is not the same for the guards (who will fight her if she arouses their suspicion), sailors, or dockworkers, who may treat her harshly if they aren't amenable to her charms, such as when she's on a mission on their turf.

My informal experiment sought to map out how the citizens generally perceive Aveline in her different guises. The vast majority of the responses I elicited were in French; I only noted two in English, both when in the guise of the slave. In Nouvelle Orléans a man warned that I was "courting a beating," and a guard on Chichen Itza declared, "Remember your place; I won't tell you twice." In short, the citizens of New Orleans treat Aveline with the utmost contempt when she is dressed as a slave; with ridiculous, saccharine deference when she is a lady; and with a mixture of fear, hostility, and resentment when she is the assassin. Shoulder-checking someone while wearing the assassin's costume, a tri-cornered hat, trousers and waistcoat, might elicit responses that range from the trepidatiously polite "Ô, je suis maladroite, excusez moi" [Oh, how clumsy I am, excuse me] or "Je m'occupe de mes af-faires" [I'm minding my own business], to the more overtly fearful "Pitié, laissez-moi partir" [Please, let me go] and the somewhat ri-diculous "Pas le visage!" [Not the face!], to the much nastier "Vous êtes aveugle?" [Are you blind?] and braver "Hors de mon chemin!" [Out of my way!]. The player who doesn't speak French can tell much about the community's reaction just from the tones of voice. Many of the people accosted in this way just cry out, wave their arms, and flee in another direction. No translation necessary. But I solicited the help of an undergraduate research assistant who does not speak French to get his read on the gestures. He was unable to distinguish the nuance in how the townspeople treat the slave and the assassin, characterizing both reactions as "hostile," though the apologetic manner in which they treat the lady was obvious to him. He also noted that "random men greet Aveline" in the lady guise where they don't when she's in the other two costumes. But being able to understand snatches of in-game dialogue reveals much more about the society's perception of Aveline's personae.

For example, some have suggested that the assassin's costume might be read as transgender, and it is evident from these encoun-ters that the people don't quite know what to make of Aveline in this guise.[2] One woman, when pushed, cries out, "Qui est cette femme?" [Who is this woman?]. At first I thought I heard her say "ce femme," which would be an incorrect use of the masculine article with the feminine, implying ambiguity. Upon more investigation, I noted that the townspeople accosted in this manner by the assassin could

2. See Jagger Gravning, "How Videogames Are Slowly, Quietly Introducing LBGT Heroes," *Atlantic*, February 25, 2014. See also Murray, "Visual Poetics."

also be prompted to exclaim, "Excuse me, Sir, eh, Madam, sorry" and to wonder aloud, "Why does she wear men's clothing?" When bumped, one man says, "Ô, seigneur, je suis desolé, desolé" [Oh, lord, I am sorry, sorry]. Is he appealing to the Lord above, or does he mistake Aveline for a nobleman here? If you approach a woman in this form she might exclaim, "Ne m'approchez pas!" [Don't come near me!]. Or you might hear, "Vous devriez avoir honte!" [You should be ashamed]. Is she fearful that the assassin could be an assailant making an attack on her virtue, or is this an accusation of some broader gender-bending impropriety? Perhaps most tellingly, these exclamations often come with insults such as "créature de malade!" [sick creature] or "demon!" Sadly, even Agaté, with whom Aveline falls out over the course of the game, ends by saying she has been "twisted . . . into this monster" and that he should have raised her as his own daughter, a repudiation of her placement in a wealthy white household. Whether this animosity is meant to be the result of Aveline's class, race, or gender transgression, I cannot say, but it is clear that the people of this world aren't sure what to make of her. Yet, despite hurling these horrible epithets at Aveline, they still address her with the formal "vous" whereas in the slave costume she is only ever addressed with the informal "tu," signifying her inferior status.

Addressed sometimes as "Esclave" and other times as "Femme" when dressed as a slave, Aveline's nudging of the crowd garners direct insults that translate to "Open your eyes, slave!," "Watch where you're going, woman!," and "Pay attention!" The gentlest responses I encountered were an exasperated, "[How about] a little calm, woman?" and "A little respect?" The townspeople are clearly indignant to see this behavior from an enslaved person, claiming "I'll teach you some good manners!" or "I ought to have you whipped!" Some accuse her of being drunk; others wonder if she's a pickpocket. She is called a "type of vermin" by one person, and another vows not to waste his time on her "kind." None of this may be directly surprising, but it is ironic when contrasted with the responses of the seemingly identical cast of anonymous townspeople when they encounter the same behavior from the same woman wearing a different dress. In this case they bend over backward to take the blame on themselves for the collision: "Veuillez m'excuser, madamoiselle," "Veuillez accepter toutes mes excuses," "Pardonnez-moi, madame." Even when I walked directly up to someone and shoved them, they said things like, "Je ne vous ai pas vue" [I didn't see you], "I'm sorry, truly!," or "Our paths crossed." My personal favorite, which is delivered in a deferent tone without a hint of passive aggressivity, is "J'ai juste ce qu'il faut pour faire disparaître ces bleus" [I have just the thing to get rid of these bruises].

Even with subtitles on, only cut-scenes include the translation of foreign languages, leaving comments such as these as well as the French greetings, asides, and snatches of overheard dialogue entirely untranslated. Although the player isn't handicapped by a language barrier in *Liberation,* a knowledge of French will heighten understanding of certain aspects of the game, particularly how the community views and treats Aveline. I also acknowledge that there may yet be more to Aveline's story that I am missing—several times I was unable to make out what a passing person said to me. It's entirely possible that there are other languages here, such as African dialects or Creoles. (One slave the player interacts with says that he is Fon and is eager to return to Africa, which may be a clue to some of the other languages heard in the game.) But I'll leave this topic aside with this last note about the use of speech in *Liberation.* Flagging the use of language as important in the game, in one instance, a smuggler named Roussillion tries to pronounce a Kreyol word "houng—haung—" and then opts for its (insufficient) translation, "witchdoctor." The word he was looking for was "houngan." This word and a few other untranslated, unexplained concepts, like "loas," signifying Vodun divinities, point to how language makes communities, even within the society of gamers.

In brief, my argument here is that although the uses of untranslated language may be a trademark of the Assassin's Creed series that lends to its historical realism, it works to particular effect in *Liberation* and *Freedom Cry* by emphasizing how a game can stratify the gamership, using a sieve-like mechanism to allow some to pass (to the next level or to a deeper understanding) and blocking the path of others in a manner that speaks specifically to the poetics of resistance. The issue of audience, that the videogame changes depending on who is playing it, is intrinsic to the medium, but it takes on new complication in games about ownership of racial history and heritage, something which the makers of Assassin's Creed, a series about people reliving their ancestors' memories, must surely be aware.[3] The polyglotism of these games strikes me as an acknowledgment of this fact: players will have dissimilar experiences interacting with these narratives. (Perhaps Aveline's diverse persona system is even meant to suggest this as well, if only in part.) This division of the audience via the incorporation of diverse languages creates a stratification in the gamership. Those fluent in French may understand the comments in the street or the ambient noise of overheard conversations in town, while others may miss the significance of words spoken in French. Nevertheless, this is a productive division that calls to mind the semiotics of slave revolt encountered in other digital games we've investigated here: the lamp in a window, the monkey wrench quilt, or the song about a drinking gourd, symbols to some but not legible to all.

In *Freedom Cry,* the use of untranslated language emphasizes the subject matter of slave revolt. The game dialogue incorporates not only French, the language of the colonists present in Saint Domingue, but also Haitian Kreyol and even some phrases from a Trinidadian dialect. As in *Liberation,* foreign languages in gameplay are untranslated even if the player turns on the subtitles. In the cut-scenes, use of foreign languages are more spare, but with subtitles on, there is a translation in brackets (such as [Bully!]), but no transliteration of the word heard (in this case "Baa John") or

3. The dangers of the game's rendering ownership of black resistance to a wide audience is a thorny issue, and not one I'm equipped to tackle. This broad "problem of white gaming" is handled more deftly in Gray and Mazurek, "Visualizing Blackness."

any indication of what language the character has spoken (here, Trinidadian Creole). As such, untranslated language lends a kind of mystery to the game, like a door through which the player is not permitted to walk. But the thing about this type of door is that certain players are permitted to pass if they speak the language.

In *Freedom Cry,* the first instance of Haitian Kreyol is heard from the slave whom Adewalé saves from deformation by the overseer. In answer to his question about how to find Bastienne Joseph, she utters a phrase that I would transliterate as "Mwen menm pa l'konnen" [Me personally? I don't know her]. In today's Haitian Kreyòl, this would be "Mwen menm, m pa konnen li," but the bracketed translation is insufficient here—it says only ["Of course not!"]. I'm not exactly sure what accounts for the difference in the Kreyol, but a woman in her nineties whom I spoke to in Port-au-Prince suggested to me that this phrase might be "La Creole Ancienne." It was what her father spoke, she told me, a creole "plus françisé." Sometimes the slaves whom Adewalé frees thank him in English, sometimes in French, and sometimes in what sounds like Kreyol. There were times at which I couldn't tell if what I was hearing was French, French spoken with a heavy African accent, Kreyol, or an older Creole. For one scene in particular, at the Maroon hideout, I enlisted the help of other French speakers and of Kreyol-speaking Haitians, and truthfully, I could get no consensus on whether the passages in question—in which Adewalé eavesdrops on conversations, one seemingly a bawdy discussion about a woman, and another about a drunkard—were in French or Creole or some hybrid. I even made attempts to contact the dialect coach who worked on the game, but the truth is that I prefer to leave this matter a mystery, for the game designers' choice to leave speech indecipherable or untranslated works as effectively, regardless. It's a productive blockage that points to the history beyond the game as one that cannot be effectively translated into a playable narrative.

Although I object to the uses of Haiti made in the incorporation of Makandal in *Liberation,* and the commodification of Saint Domingue's legacy of slave resistance in *Freedom Cry,* I want to

acknowledge here another perspective. In a review on the site
Kotaku, Haitian American games journalist Evan Narcisse writes,

> Never in a million years did I ever think I'd hear Haitian Kreyol in a
> video game. And yet, there it was in *Freedom Cry*, as lilting and per-
> cussive as when my mom spoke it. For the few hours I steered Ade-
> walé through his saga, I didn't feel horribly under-represented or
> taken for granted in the medium I write about. It's a feeling I could
> use more of.[4]

In this review, Narcisse makes several good points about the game,
for example its deft avoidance of Vaudou, a topic that is too often
used to ignorantly demonize the culture, and its incorporation of
authentic Haitian music. At the outset, Narcisse claims the game
for himself: "The newest chapter of the Assassin's Creed series
gives me some of the things I've always wanted in a videogame:
a heroic fantasy that lets me control a warrior fighting against
slavery." One of the ways the game invites Narcisse to feel that the
game is *for* him and his Haitian heritage rather than a shallow appropriation of it are these shibboleths, like the songs he recogniz-
es, or the phrases others might.[5]

There are other instances where uses of Kreyol explicitly divide
the gamership into those in the know, who can understand the exchange on a deeper meaning, and those who don't, who are, effectively, left out of the joke. There are two separate occasions when
characters in the game, an unnamed freed slave and Madame
Josephe, refer to Adewalé as "Blanc," the Haitian word for stranger that translates literally to "white person." Although the player
who reads the translation provided ([foreigner]) if captions are

---

4. Evan Narcisse, "A Game That Showed Me My Own History,"
Kotaku, December 19, 2013, http://kotaku.com/a-game-that-showed-me-my
-own-black-history-1486643518.
5. Although it concerns the Lakota playing a game about the Mohawk
people and therefore doesn't share the language concerns, see Joe Flood,
"Playing *Assassin's Creed 3* on the Pine Ridge Rez," *Killscreen,* November 28,
2012 for a discussion of some of the same issues I explore here.

enabled might understand that this indicates that the characters do not fully trust Adewalé, he or she would still likely miss the irony of their referring to the black Adewalé as "white" and all that this term implies in reference to the culture's sense of solidarity. Because of the society's general division into an upper-class caste of mixed-race descendants of the colonists and the impoverished free blacks and slaves, this term is fraught with history.

The inclusion of a password early in the game suggests that the game designers were thoughtful in their use of untranslated language. When Adewalé first meets with the intended recipient of the parcel he bears, she gives him a task to prove his trustworthiness. So that he might find his way to the Maroon hideout to deliver a message, Bastienne teaches Adewalé to sing a snippet of song to the field slaves as a passcode to gain access and information. The song is a line from a traditional Haitian lullaby, "Si ou pa dodo crab la va manje w," which roughly translates to "If you don't go to sleep, the crab will eat you." While it is true that recognizing that the song is a lullaby and knowing what it means don't seem to further understanding of the game, its inclusion here acknowledges that the use of language in the game acts as a kind of password, permitting some players to accede to a different level of understanding.

The interactivity of the structure of the videogame is a complex element in depictions of slave revolt: it can allow a game developer to control historical narratives of slave resistance, reducing matters of deep historical importance to entertainment. As we've seen, game texts can also work in a productive manner that emphasizes that such a narrative may speak differently to gamers of diverse ancestry by restricting the player's access to the full story through the use of language or requiring a labor of cultural recognition on the part of the player to unlock parts of the story. It's not that these games wholly manage to avoid problematic commodification of black resistance or a troubling appropriation of historical slave revolt, but in certain ways, they employ subversive tactics in a productive manner.

Failure and *Freedom Cry*

UP TO THIS POINT, we've looked at how specific games hold open an aporia that can productively be read as safeguarding the untraversable space of history. But for this study to be complete, we must also account for the complication inherent in rendering this history in an interactive form. This demands that we climb into a thorny thicket: we must question, if only to ultimately disagree with, the supposition that the videogaming form speaks to the themes of slavery and revolt. Or, more succinctly put, we must ask, is the videogame an apt space in which to dramatize this history?

As Bernard Perron and Mark Wolf note in their introduction to the second *Video Game Theory Reader,* this is a medium that "actively *resists* analysis by withholding itself from those who do not have the skills to keep their avatars alive."[1] Therefore, the mode of the videogame may offer something that a text like literature or film cannot: it will push back against the player in a felt, concrete matter. One might argue that typical functions of the videogaming form echo the strict restraint the enslaved faced and that the tension between the player, who would deftly navigate the world of the game, and the game developer's algorithm, which limits and challenges the player, acts as some kind of formalist analogy to enslavement. Maybe, in some ways, these games recall in their form as well as in their content the restrictions placed on the historical slave. But it's *only* a game.

Nonetheless, here is how this argument goes: when the player bumps into immovable objects or feels the frustration of a disen-

1. Bernard Perron and Mark J. P. Wolf, eds., *The Video Game Theory Reader 2* (New York: Routledge, 2009), 6. Emphasis added.

abled button, *(no, that object on the table cannot be picked up, but this one can)*, he or she feels like a disempowered figure within the larger institution of the programmer's world, "experiencing the algorithm," in Galloway's parlance, or the defamiliarizing effects of the videogame, in Holger Pötzsch's terms.[2] When the player fails a level and must repeat it for the fifteenth time by going rote through the steps *(cut the rope, jump across the loose board, grab the lasso and swing to the other side of the bridge before its collapse)*—what the kids today call "grinding"—the player performs a kind of labor to get to the next level. All videogames are about both power and powerlessness and work and play. As Tom Bissell says, in videogames, "You get control and are controlled."[3] The dyad of the player's control and lack of control has been much discussed by videogame scholars, but as I'm not trying to argue here for its importance to videogames about historical slavery, I'll leave this aside for the moment, with one last note.[4] I concede that videogames about slavery and slave revolt showcase the medium's inherent dialectics (between puissance and impotence, pleasure and pain, work and leisure) as we experience our own push and pull as subjects within the computer system in a new, troubling, light.

2. Galloway, *Gaming,* 19. Pötzsch argues that "particular devices are deployed with the objective to de-familiarize, problematize, and challenge taken for granted perspectives and conventions" in videogames just as "Brecht's plays use devices of estrangement" in theater (8).

3. Tom Bissell, *Extra Lives: Why Video Games Matter,* rev ed. (New York: Vintage Books, 2011), 39.

4. Jesper Juul identifies rules as "the most consistent source of player enjoyment in games" (*Half-Real,* 55). Galloway writes of the controlling algorithm of the videogame structure, of the way that, on some level, all videogames are about control and the mechanisms of control in place in our contemporary society. When we confront the "algorithm" in games, he argues, witnessing their strict ordering, we are called to think about this aspect of our own world (gaming). On player choice and agency, see also Sebastien Domsch, *Storyplaying: Agency and Narrative in Videogames* (Berlin: De Gruyter, 2013).

I want to be clear here that I am not arguing that the form of videogames approximates slavery and revolt—though I can see how one might interpret this element of videogame construction as conducive to dramatizing narratives about slavery. Videogames about slavery and revolt operate in a peculiar register because to play a videogame is to be incarnated into a world simultaneously in one's control and not in one's control. To play a videogame is to explore the borders of its structural mechanisms, to identify its rules, and to find the power to overcome its limits.[5] The dialectics of power inherent in gameplay regarding the struggle between the game developer and the player, or the gamer and the game, might seem to take on new resonances when the narrative at hand concerns the agency of the rebel slave. However, I would emphasize that the performance of slavery in such games offers a richer—in that it operates within both the narrative and ludic registers—but also more potentially *problematic*, experience of role-playing.[6]

5. In *Half-Real*, Jesper Juul writes, "gameplay is an interaction between the rules and the player's attempt at playing the game as well as possible" (56). See also Jesper Juul, "Fear of Failing? The Many Meanings of Difficulty in Video Games" in *The Video Game Theory Reader 2*, edited by Bernard Perron and Mark J. P. Wolf (New York: Routledge, 2009), 237–52 and Jesper Juul, *The Art of Failure. An Essay on the Pain of Playing Video Games* (Cambridge, Mass.: MIT Press, 2013).

6. For example, there are complications inherent in such games' offering of the occupation of the black body to variously embodied gamers, allowing a kind of racial cross-dressing or even blackface in the form of avatars, what Lisa Nakamura called "identity tourism." Lisa Nakamura, "Race In/For Cyberspace: Identity Tourism and Racial Passing on the Internet," *Works and Days: Essays in the Socio-Historical Dimensions of Literature and the Arts*, 25/26 (Fall 1995, Winter 1996): 181–93. See also Anna Everett, *Digital Diaspora: A Race for Cyberspace* (Albany, N.Y.: SUNY University Press, 2009) and Anna Everett and Craig Watkins, "The Power of Play: The Portrayal and Performance of Race in Video Games," in *The Ecology of Games: Connecting Youth, Games, and Learning*, edited by Katie Salen (Cambridge, Mass.: MIT Press, 2008), 141–66. Kishonna Grey seems like one of the most recent productive scholars on the topic of audience participation and race. See Kishonna Grey, *Race, Gender, and Deviance in Xbox Live: Theoretical Perspectives from the Virtual Margins* (New York:

Instead, I'm arguing that these same limitations inherent to the form can be seen as productively *withholding* history from the player, prohibiting a complete absorption into the character.

It is as if the rigid gaming structure presents the possibility of the player's identification with the historically enslaved person only to ultimately refute this as a viable option. The games about historical slavery that interest me are those that work on the level of the closed door, the blocked path, the interrupted mission, the failed level. These devices, what Soraya Murray would call the games' *poetics,* represent the potential of the player's occupation of the historical personage of the slave-in-revolt but, ultimately, obstruct in important ways the completion of that transformation. Therefore, my conclusion is this: the player's sense of his or her own limitations within the system is not meant to *mirror* the enslaved person's real-life oppression, but rather to *resist* the contemporary player's occupation of that role. Although the restriction of choice and other aspects of gameplay may seem to work to particular effect (and affect) in games about slavery and resistance, I want to paraphrase James Sweeting's discussion of the game *Spec Ops: The Line*: "the player . . . has one *real* choice: whether to play the game." Any conflation between these ludic texts and the reality of the enslaved is patently absurd.[7]

Routledge, 2014). For a discussion of game mechanics and race, see Alison Reed and Amanda Phillips, "Additive Race: Colorblind Discourses of Realism in Performance Capture Technologies," *Digital Creativity* 24, no. 2 (2013): 130–44. Soraya Murray takes a critical race studies position within videogame studies in *On Videogames: The Visual Politics of Race, Gender, and Space* (London: I.B. Taurus, 2017), as does Tanner Higgin, "Gamic Race: Logics of Difference in Videogame Culture" (PhD diss., University of California Riverside, 2012).

    7. Sweeting is discussing the way that *Spec Ops: The Line* uses illusory choice to make a point about videogame play; here, I have stressed the word *real* because the games that I'm investigating remind the player of his or her separation from the lived historical reality of the characters he or she digitally inhabits. In Sweeting, the line reads, "the player only has one real choice: whether to play the game." Sweeting, "Illusions of Choice."

On this front, we might consider moments of "selective interactivity" (for example, when pushing a certain button on a controller suddenly stops having the desired effect) and "operationalized weakness" (like Aveline's limitations when wearing a particular guise) as reminders of the player's distance from the PC. But even more importantly, some of these games withhold mastery from the player tout court.[8] This has already been alluded to in the discussion of some games' lack of a satisfying conclusion, but it is evidenced most concretely in the end of *Freedom Cry*.

Strikingly, *Freedom Cry* denies the player the possibility of accomplishing the task at hand in a heart-wrenching scene near the end of the game. Adewalé and the Maroons have begun to attack incoming slave ships to the island with the hope of freeing the slaves even before they arrive. The embattled French Gouverneur de Fayet, angered by the major losses in his workforce that the rebel slaves have cost him by breaking into cages in the public square, interrupting slave auctions, and the other such "missions" that comprise the gameplay, orders the French to fire on and sink a slave ship, causing major loss of life rather than allowing this human cargo to go free and be, as is Adewalé's goal, recruited to the ever-growing Maroon army. The governor's act of immense cruelty may call to mind the *Zong* massacre of 1781, in which the captain threw 132 enslaved people overboard so that he could seek reimbursement for their value by filing an insurance claim.[9]

Adewalé boards the sinking ship, but he cannot possibly save all the slaves. This is a deeply unsetting part of the game, as it rapidly

8. For discussion on selective interactivity, see Bogost, *Persuasive Games*, 46; for operationalized weakness, see Bogost, *How to Do*, 20.

9. See Ian Baucom, *Specters of the Atlantic: Finance Capital, Slavery, and the Philosophy of History* (Durham, N.C.: Duke University Press, 2005) in which the author sets out a theory of history derived from Édouard Glissant and Walter Benjamin, which he calls "accumulated history." Baucom uses the *Zong* massacre as a pivotal point in this articulation. See also Ian Baucom, "Specters of the Atlantic," *South Atlantic Quarterly* 100, no. 1 (Winter 2001).

switches back and forth between scripted cut-scenes over which the player has no control and shorter episodes in which the player retains command of the PC. In this part of the game, the second to last mission, the hero is bound to fail, as it is impossible to unlock all of the slaves' shackles before the boat sinks. Although Adewalé later assassinates the governor as retribution for his heartless act, this penultimate mission tinges the rest of the game with a sense of failure and loss.

In this part of the gameplay, after boarding the sinking ship, the player moves to the hull and attempts to free as many slaves as possible. Frustratingly, each set of slave's irons requires a different manipulation of the buttons, which must be learned on the fly. This is a perfect example of the kind of defamiliarization device that Holger Pötzsch describes as creating estrangement in the world of the videogame.[10] His reading of these devices emphasizes the player's separation from the game as resulting in "a source of innovative player engagement beyond a ludic or immersive attitude that makes the very rules and mechanics structuring interaction and perception the potential object of critical inquiry, politically inflected discussions, and formal intervention." That is, as in Brechtian theatre, the estrangement from the world of the game may bring about the most essential aspects of its critique. Moments where the game becomes visible as a game break the player's immersion to remind him of his distance from the PC. Otherwise, this can be achieved through frustration, as previously noted, and even failure.

Tension mounts as the people shackled to the sinking ship scream in terror and the water level rises. After freeing some of them, the player is forced by the programmed directives to escape, leaving behind the rest. No longer capable of interacting with the doomed figures, the player must leap or swim over the drowning people to

---

10. Pötzsch writes that "A deliberate de-familiarizing of game controls is one viable option to achieve such effects." Pötzsch, "Playing Games," 10.

climb through the ship, now vertical in its pitch, before it submerges. The mission ends with a cut-scene on the beach, where the PC meets with his fellow renegades to bury the dead. There, Adewalé admits to feeling guilt since it was his action that caused the governor to behave so drastically and vows to kill him. This is fulfilled in the next and last mission, in which the governor is assassinated in the act of torturing a slave with a branding iron. In the denouement, Adewalé tells Bastienne that he has determined to devote the rest of his life to fighting for the freedom of his people, but there is little sense of victory permitted. As the final credits roll, the mood is sorrowful. This example may seem similar to the case mentioned previously from the educational game *Mission US,* where options are foreclosed when the PC is sold on the auction block, giving the player an approximation of the lack of choice involved in slavery and no course of action for defying it. Therefore, one answer to the question raised above about what makes videogames an apt form in which to discuss such a difficult historical topic, is that they can refuse the player admittance to certain aspects, withhold identification with the historic subject, or deny victory and thereby refuse to yield mastery over the rebel slave.

Freedom Cry, like other games we've discussed here, seems to willfully deprive the player any celebratory rhetoric in a manner befitting a game about slavery. We might think of the Maroon leader Augustin Dieufort's last words in the game, spoken on the beach as he helps bury the drowned slaves that Adewalé could not free, as an indication of how it operates in relation to the history it represents. Dieufort says of the dead, "We will always mourn them." As much as this game celebrates a legacy of slave resistance, it is at the same time an act of cultural mourning for the transatlantic slave trade. The game's mechanics, including the type of operationalized weakness on display in this mission, drive home the nuanced difficulty of creating a game that takes as its subject matter the historical modes of oppression and resistance of the enslaved. It risks, in its formal composition, a collapsing of the player and the historical character he or she pilots across the landscape. To make a game such as this one *winnable* would risk offering the player a catharsis. Refusing this possibility is a productive acknowledgment of how we remain haunted by the "specters of the Atlantic," in Ian Baucom's phrase.

Therein, the game defies players' expectations and forecloses the possibility of triumph. My, perhaps charitable, reading of this conclusion is that it safeguards the history of the rebel slave as one ultimately inaccessible to the player, but I can imagine an alternate reading that could accuse the game designers of cowardice. The same company allowed the feminine, mixed-race Aveline to conquer her foes, but the black male character is denied either optimism or victory in the end. However, I would argue that aspects of the game are even more intriguing when they reveal effects unplanned by the designer.

Freedom Cry, a game about personal agency and the prehistory of the slave revolt of Saint Domingue (which, as we know from Susan Buck-Morss's foundational essay "Hegel and Haiti," was the spark for Hegel's theory of the Master/Slave dialectic) may seem an apt setting for the articulation of the videogame player's dialectic of power and powerlessness, to which all videogames might be said to contribute. As Frans Mäyrä has said, games are "not static objects," so this boundary line—that slash between controlled/controlling—is ever in flux.[11] This dialectic seeks to define the boundary between the player's capacity for co-creation of the game narrative and the rigid compartmentalization of his role by the game designer. But it's more complicated, even, than this. Aspects of the game like unavoidable failure, operationalized weakness, and selective interactivity are plainly part of the algorithm installed by the developer, but more broadly, videogames are complex texts that not only restrict

11. Frans Mäyrä, "Getting into the Game: Doing Multidisciplinary Game Studies," in *The Video Game Theory Reader 2,* edited by Bernard Perron and Mark J. P. Wolf (New York: Routledge, 2009), 313–29. See also Frans Mäyrä, *An Introduction to Game Studies: Games in Culture* (London: SAGE publications, 2008).

the freedom and movement of the player but sometimes exceed the developer's control in a manner that further problematizes the dialectic of control and controlled.

The line between the controlled and the controlling will shift within a game as it will from player to player, and it is determined not merely by the developer's choices or the player's skill but also by external circumstances. Mods, hacks, glitches, and other phenomena that exist in the broader space of online fan community are part of play. A brief digression on the subject of glitches and fan communities in *Freedom Cry* highlights the complexity of player agency, making clear what Boluk and Lemieux write in their book *Metagaming*: "there are no glitches, nothing is out of bounds."[12] Identifying such moments, where the game exceeds not only the player's abilities but also the developer's intentions, illustrates another way in which the videogame seems uniquely suited as a venue to stage discussions of the complex history of slave revolt.

For example, in one sequence of the game *Freedom Cry*, the player is instructed that the next mission will be to liberate Wellington plantation in the Caribbean. For some reason, though, the mission icon, an exclamation point directing the player to the site, is greyed out and the mission therefore reads as locked. Previously in the game, there was a similar challenge where the player had to liberate 150 slaves before advancing to the next mission.[13] Although the only thing that the player actually must do is to set a course for the plantation and destroy the slave ships encountered on the way in order to reach Wellington, there appears to be a kind of design error here. Whereas the typical convention is that a mission unlocks

12. The authors elaborate on this point: "If videogames are agnostic to how they are played and every operation yields states of equal value, then there are no glitches, nothing is out of bounds, and the intentions of an author and audience are a completely arbitrary metagame in and of themselves." Boluk and Lemieux, *Metagaming*, 46.

13. Perhaps this error has subsequently been fixed, but this was my experience when playing the DLC game in 2017. As of this writing, there are still several threads visible online in which gamers discuss this problem.

when the player is ready to undertake it, the Wellington plantation mission only visibly unlocks *after* it is liberated. Staring at the
icon, I made the assumption that I did not yet have the capacity to
attack the plantation, and I was not alone in my confusion about
what to do in this situation.

An internet rumor states that you must liberate five hundred
slaves in order to unlock the mission, and I, and many other poor
rubes whose lamenting I found in online gaming forums, under-
took to do just that. By falling prey to this trap, the act of liberating
slaves becomes horribly tiresome. Five hundred is a lot, especially
as there are only a set number of scenarios that can be replayed in
Port-au-Prince, each garnering one or two or, most of the time, a
handful of emancipated slaves. The player must run around the
island, encountering the same few sequences over and over: buying slaves (with money looted from kills, mainly), violently freeing
slaves on the auction block, letting captives out of a locked pen,
chasing down an overseer following a fleeing slave, carrying a sick
person to safety, or freeing a plantation without the guards sound-
ing the alarm bells. Though this rumor is *not* a planned part of
gameplay, it nonetheless works well for the theme of the game, on
several levels. Firstly, it encourages a feeling of frustration from the
forced repetition and powerlessness and maybe a sense of irony, if
the player lamenting the fact that the act of freeing the enslaved
has become tiresome *work* is capable of enough self-awareness to
realize that he or she is feeling constrained and oppressed by a
digital game played as a leisure activity.

Interestingly, then, games seem to work subversively (in this
instance and others) by *not working*. At one point, in my personal
experience with *Freedom Cry,* there was a level in which I fulfilled
all the obligations to succeed in my mission to free a plantation's
worth of slaves, but I was glitched out of the reward I was due.
The game system refused to recognize that I *had* the key I needed
to open the door to the slaves' prison, and I was unable to save the
level without resolving the issue. We might read this unfairness
as the game's seditious malfunctioning, which works to highlight

the injustice of the system against which the protagonist struggles. But even more profitably, such moments reveal the ghost in the machine—by which I mean, the game itself taking on life beyond the game developer's plans—and becoming a kind of third author of the game. The glitch is a part of the magic circle.[14]

As such, this medium may offer us a useful space in which to have a conversation about the representation of slave resistance in art. Who is qualified to author narratives of slave resistance, particularly when a fiction dialogues with historical reality? The level of care that must be demonstrated in treating the subject matter is exemplified in the case of William Styron's highly controversial 1967 novel *The Confessions of Nat Turner*. Although Styron's book earned a Pulitzer Prize, it was followed by an immense backlash that resulted in the publication of a book called *Ten Black Writers Respond*. In brief, Styron's depiction of Nat Turner as a man whose motives for his infamous rebellion were contaminated by his obsession with a white woman was seen as trafficking in stereotypes. The communal production of videogames, which may include not only a team of designers and developers but also the metagaming of fan communities and even design flaws, complicates the issue of who is qualified to depict slave resistance in art. The fact that this medium allows not only for pushback against the player but also, in some cases, resistance to the developer's intentions, signals that no one owns slave revolt. The game not only resists the player's absorption in the narrative, but it also rebels against the developer's construction of it in a manner that is suited for such a fraught history.

14. For a discussion of the magic circle of play, a concept first discussed by Johan Huizinga in his 1938 *Homo Ludens: A Study of the Play-Element in Culture* and how this idea has evolved in game theory, see Dominic Arsenault and Bernard Perron, "In the Frame of the Magic Circle: The Circle(s) of Gameplay," in *The Video Game Theory Reader 2,* edited by Bernard Perron and Mark J. P. Wolf (New York: Routledge, 2009), 109–31. See also Katie Salen and Eric Zimmerman, *Rules of Play: Game Design Fundamentals* (Cambridge, Mass.: MIT Press, 2004).

A Digital Fragment

THE ARTISTIC VIDEOGAME *Thralled* has been publicly anticipated at least since 2013, when it was profiled in Evan Narcisse's article on the website Kotaku with the title, "I Need This Haunting Game about a Runaway Slave to Get Finished."[1] Created by students at the University of Southern California Games Innovation Lab, *Thralled* seems to be in a direct lineage of serious games like *Papers, Please, Darfur is Dying,* and particularly *Hush,* which is about a Rwandan mother who must quiet her child to avoid detection by soldiers.[2] Those interested in the game can access the mission statement and trailer on the game's website, Thralled.org, and limited play-throughs and student demonstrations are available on YouTube, but downloadable playable content is not available anywhere to date. Rather than being a detriment, the game's unfinishedness and limited accessibility seem to work in tandem with its theme of rebellion. The unreleased fragment *Thralled* acts as a non-game, somewhat like Brenda Romero's material game about the slave trade, *The New World.*[3]

1. Evan Narcisse, "I Really Need This Haunting Game about a Runaway Slave to Get Finished," Kotaku, August 2013, https://kotaku.com/i-really-need-this-creepy-game-about-a-runaway-slave-to-1184668918.

2. On *Papers, Please,* see Matthew Kelly, "The Game of Politics: Examining the Role of Work, Play, and Subjectivity Formation in *Papers, Please," Games and Culture* 13, no. 5 (2015): 459–78. See also Bogost, *Persuasive Games* and Katherine Isbister, *How Games Move Us: Emotion by Design* (Cambridge, Mass.: MIT Press, 2016) for discussion of "serious games."

3. For more on Brenda Romero's work, see her discussion of her games both at "Gaming for Understanding – Brenda Brathwaite," posted on August 21, 2013, Ted Talk, 9:23, https://www.youtube.com/watch?v=lH83NyjoXbU and "G4C13 Keynote: Brenda Romero," posted on June 26, 2013, YouTube video, 23:11, https://www.youtube.com/watch?v=AzQMcKArcYU.

Romero's *The New World* is not a purchasable commodity but rather an installation exhibit in which the "player" must load wooden pegs representing people onto a slave ship. Romero's game about the Holocaust, *Train,* operates in a similar way. The player only discovers later in the game that the trains are bound for concentration camps, perhaps encouraging a feeling of complicity. As non-games, Romero's works call into question expectations about player agency and games' ability to foster empathy for the historical people represented by the wooden pegs. Expectations of ludic form and empathy are likewise raised by *Thralled,* and just as Romero's "games" cannot be purchased, this game about a runaway slave remains an incomplete and largely inaccessible digital fragment.

The developers were kind enough to send me a playable version of the first chapter as a demo, and it is my experience with this version that I'll present here. *Thralled* is a side-scrolling puzzle game in which the player pilots the small figure of Isaura across the landscape. On a black screen, the opening frames inform the player of the historical context of the game:

> Between 1500 and 1888, an estimated 12 million African men, women, and children were forcibly taken from their homes and sold as slaves in the Americas . . . The majority of these Africans were taken to the Portuguese colony of Brazil and forced to work on its sugarcane plantations . . . Among them was Isaura.

As the title cards share this information, the player hears the sound of a dense rain falling. When the last words dissolve, the sound of a baby crying—a sound which the player of this game must grow accustomed to—is introduced as the image of Isaura holding her child at the foot of a giant mangrove tree fades in. Supertitles situate the action: "Pernambuco, Brazil, 1700s." The rain falls on Isaura and her baby until the player begins the action by shushing the child, a gesture that will become a frequent and urgent one. No instruction is given to the player, and I've found in the various classes in which I've demoed this game that students often begin with a feeling of what Gilleade and Dix call in-game frustration "when an objective is not given."[4] It's only once they've figured out through trial and error that pushing the space bar will effect Isaura's soothing of the babe that the gameplay properly starts, at which point the perspective zooms out and the haunting humming of the game's soundtrack begins. At this point, the player has control of Isaura and must move her from the left to the right of the screen, helping her to cross the terrain, remove obstacles, and use objects along the way to make her path easier in this two-dimensional platformer game. She can backtrack only a certain distance; a waterfall appears to the left of the screen that marks the point of no return.

Let me begin by saying, candidly, that unlike other side-scrolling puzzle games I've played, there is absolutely nothing even remotely enjoyable about *Thralled*. In fact, the persistent crying of the infant makes this chapter an anxiety-filled agony. In particularly tense moments, other equally piercing sounds intrude into the aural space, including a frequent metallic screech something like the braying of a donkey and eerie music that elicited gooseflesh the first dozen times I played the level. (Members of my household begged me to mute the game, but I felt that was cheating.) The most intense moments come when Isaura arrives at locations that she cannot traverse while holding the baby, such as a high rockface that needs to be scaled. She must then find a designated safe-zone (a bower) in which to lay the baby down while she accomplishes a task that allows them to cross, like performing a complicated set of maneuvers to use an overturned wagon as a step ladder. The entire time that the baby is not in Isaura's arms, he wails discomfortingly for his mother. And as if this wasn't stressful enough, there's also the apparition to worry about.

Called the "Reflection" by the developers in a demo of an early version of the game, this figure is a pale, somewhat transparent woman who looks something like Isaura's white double. The two women are of the same relative size, but the Reflection is ashen,

---

4. Gilleade and Dix, "Using Frustration," 230.

her dress is more detailed, and she wears no headscarf, whereas Isaura's dress evokes the traditional Bahian costume worn by slave women in the north of Brazil, with a belling skirt and headwrap.[5] Ghostly, or witch-like, the specter pursues Isaura as she crosses the jungle. If the wailing child is left too long in the bower, the apparition reaches him, and her touch causes the game to end. As she draws closer to the baby, sounds warn that time is running out, which only heightens the player's stress. The ghost's approach is signaled by a clanking mechanical sound possibly meant to evoke the grinding of the wheels in the sugarcane mill. The apparition may represent the white colonizers who separated Isaura and her child, or she may recall the ancestral spirits from the world of the dead. In fact, this conflation reminds us that some Africans sold to European slavers confused the white slavers for ghosts because entities from the hereafter were thought to be pale.[6] If the Reflection touches the baby, the entire level must be replayed from the start. If the player finishes the task at hand and reaches the baby before the white woman, the player still has to successfully quiet his cries or else the Reflection can claim him, a fact that makes comforting the baby quickly a crucial skill. Therefore, the game consists of often having to replay the level and repeat the same gestures—for my part, in a frenzied manner, my nerves frayed by the sounds of the baby's cries and the tense auditory signals of the Reflection's approach, which add to the dread of what will happen if this isn't done fast enough. For one, it means suffering through this same routine once more.

By the admission of the creators in their game demo presentation, this insistence on repetition emphasizes the labor of the

5. That the reflection is specifically meant to represent "a dead version of the main character" is stated in Carmichael, "Empathy Game."

6. See the discussion of the Kongolese *vumbi* in Adam Hochschild, *King Leopold's Ghost: A Story of Greed, Terror, and Heroism in Colonial Africa* (Boston: Houghton Mifflin, 1998).

enslaved.[7] But the repetition resonates with the theme of slavery regarding more than just the labors that Isaura performs.[8] Repeating this level several times, the player becomes somewhat inured to the horrors that accompany the specter's approach in the first several play-throughs. The gameplay remains stressful and the game remains appropriately *un*-fun, but the player can eventually become habituated to the ghost's clattering, stalking approach. This aspect of the game emphasizes, like Katherine McKittrick's attention to the famous photograph of the slave Gordon's scarred back, most commonly called *Scourged Back,* that "if we are not very careful, the image becomes so ordinary that the pleasures of looking, again and again, incite a second order of violence."[9] That is, if we become inoculated against the horrors of the imagery through repetition, we repeat the initial violence of the slaveholder's lack of empathy. Repetition also works, of course, to represent the theme of trauma, and descriptions of later levels of the game in the developers' mission statements call into question whether Isaura is meant to be in the New World or in Africa in this first level.

Is this level a subjective depiction of Isaura's initial capture and separation from her child, or is she, as the title card suggests, in Brazil, fleeing her enslavement? What are we to make of the *nkisi,* carved wooden Kongolese fetishes that would surely be more commonly found in Africa, that punctuate the landscape she traverses, hanging from trees as if they were lynched bodies? At one point, Isaura encounters a sculpture of a mother and child posed like a

7. USC Gamepipe Laboratory, "2013 Spring Demo Day Thralled," posted May 15, 2013, YouTube video, 15:30, https://www.youtube.com/watch?v=Flf0r00rZok.

8. On the labor of serious games, see again Matthew Kelly, "Game of Politics," particularly for his discussion of "work-as-play": "the 'work' of playing a game is the intellectual investment of continual self-reflection and self-modification of one's actions or thoughts within a virtual space" (469).

9. Katherine McKittrick, "Mathematics Black Life," *Black Scholar* 44, no. 2 (Summer 2014): 16–28.

Madonna, which she would be likely to encounter in Portuguese Brazil, but its translation into the form of a carved wooden nkisi may be another indication of the game's subjective viewpoint. Is this a Catholic icon that she translates into the form of a recognizable African fetish? Of course, this first level is not the game, which makes it difficult to analyze as a stand-alone artifact, for it raises many more questions than it answers.

No matter how successfully Isaura manages to outrun the Reflection—accomplishing her tasks in a timely manner, retrieving her child from the safe-zones, and managing to soothe him and stop his heart-wrenching cries before the ghostly woman closes the distance to the infant—at the end of the first chapter Isaura emerges from an underground cavern to face her with nowhere left to run. The Reflection approaches Isaura and lays hands on the child. The capture of the mother and child is followed by a dissolve to an image of Isaura drowning beneath the water, with her child floating away from her, perhaps a metaphoric representation of her crossing the ocean to her enslavement. After this, the game title appears. This has been, it seems, a kind of preamble, suggesting that Isaura was separated from her infant even before the crossing. The representation of her escape from a plantation in Brazil may therefore be overlaid with traumatic flashbacks that signify her separation from her baby and her homeland. Perhaps, in short, she only *imagines* that she is carrying her child. The developer's description states:

> *Thralled* is an interactive experience that portrays the surreal journey of Isaura, a runaway slave separated from her newborn and tormented by memories of a painful past. Set in 18th-century Brazil, *Thralled* follows Isaura as she traverses a nightmarish representation of the New World, reliving a distorted reminiscence of life in captivity and the events that led to the taking away of her baby boy.[10]

Despite the third person perspective of this platformer, the opening level of the game is clearly marked as a subjective rendering

10. Thralled.org, https://www.thralled.org/.

of Isaura's trauma. It would seem that the player witnesses how Isaura bears with the trauma of being separated from her child and her homeland.

Regardless of whether the completed game would ultimately contradict this interpretation, the fact that the white figure cannot be eluded at the chapter's end adds much to the feeling of disempowerment that this tense, exhausting demo creates in its form as much as in its content. This first chapter, an incomplete fragment of an unreleased game, is decidedly unwinnable.

In February of 2017, I was invited to give a presentation on this and other videogames about slavery at Rensselaer Polytechnic Institute, and the developers of *Thralled* were kind enough to allow me to demo the game throughout the day at the EMPAC Center. I was fascinated by the response the game garnered. More than one game developer told me *Thralled* was "unsuccessful" because it blocked the player's absorption in the narrative. Perhaps because of its difficulty and, especially, its aural unpleasantness, it lacked what Bolter and Grusin call "immediacy," which "dictates that the medium itself should disappear and leave us in the presence of the thing represented: sitting in the race car or standing on a mountaintop."[11]

Yet, for me, this is precisely what makes this text *successful* as a game about a rebel slave. Videogames depicting slave resistance offer a potentially problematic act of occupation of the historically subjugated person when the player is invited to play *as* the enslaved. Commoditizing the rebel slave as a playable protagonist risks "eating the [historical] Other," to invoke bell hooks's description of cultural appropriation. When these games interrupt their own "immediacy" in the sense used by Bolter and Grusin, that is, when they *defy* their invisibility as a medium and instead insist upon their presence, they work against their own problematic consumption,

---

11. Jay David Bolter and Richard Grusin, *Remediation: Understanding New Media* (Cambridge, Mass.: MIT Press, 1999), 6.

reminding players of the separation between themselves and the historical subject position they would play at being. This defiance challenges how we think of empathy as fostered by interactivity.

Katherine Isbister writes that games "play a powerful role in creating empathy and other strong, positive emotional experiences."[12] While I don't disagree, I think inquiry into serious games (particularly those that represent real, lived, or living subjects) should also consider how gestures of empathy have often come with an eclipse of the Other.[13] In short, the trick is how to have empathy for others without replacing a concern for them with a concern for the self. One such way, I would suggest, is by engineering moments of non-immediacy that act as aporias, deflecting the player's complete absorption into the character's life as a reminder, in essence, that while it is only a game for the player, it was a reality for someone else.

As I said at the beginning of this section, there is evidence that the completed version of *Thralled* was highly anticipated in the press, with articles in 2013 and 2014 from *Verge, Killscreen,* and many others mentioning the title.[14] As recently as 2015, it was included on a *Motherboard*'s list of best forthcoming games, but

12. Isbister, *How Games Move Us,* xvii.

13. Saidiya Hartman, *Scenes of Subjection,* 19. See also bell hooks, "Eating the Other: Desire and Resistance," in *Black Looks: Race and Representation* (Boston: South End Press, 1992), 21–39. On "ironies of empathy," see Alisha Gaines, "A Secondhand Kind of Terror," in *From Uncle Tom's Cabin to The Help: Critical Perspectives on White-Authored Narratives of Black Life,* edited by Claire Oberon Garcia, Vershawn Ashanti Young, and Charise Pimentel (New York: Palgrave Macmillan, 2014), 159–69 and Alisha Gaines, *Black for a Day: White Fantasies of Race and Empathy* (Charlotte: University of North Carolina Press, 2017).

14. Andrew Webster, "Can an iPad Game Teach You about Slavery?" *Verge,* September 13, 2013, and Jess Joho, "How the Upcoming *Thralled* Could Help Us Better Understand the Atrocity of Slavery," *Killscreen,* March 21, 2014. The game was also profiled on *Huffington Post, Venture Beat, Gaming Bolt, Grabit Magazine,* and *J Station X.* See the "media" tab on Thralled.org for a sampling of articles mentioning or profiling the game.

that was five years ago now, and I fear that since the official website *still* lists its release date as "to be announced," that this game may never come be released.[15] Nonetheless, for our purposes here, *Thralled*'s existence as a fragment, an unfinished game, is apt. With a single completed level that forecloses victory for the player, the game seems to be among those that withhold the satisfaction of play from the wider gamership. However, the game's fragmentary state and inaccessibility, existing as this demo does as a preamble without a narrative, deprive the would-be player not only of a satisfying ending but also of even the proper game itself. The fact that *Thralled* exists mainly in press clippings and gaming lore brackets this history as not only unwinnable but even *unplayable* for the majority.

15. Zack Kotzer, "Motherboard's 15 Games to Look Forward to in 2015," Vice, January 2, 2015, https://www.vice.com/en_us/article/jp5aq4 /games-to-look-forward-to-since-the-last-guardian-is-never-coming-out. See also Colin Campbell, "Ouya Slavery Game *Thralled* Now Coming to Multiple Platforms," *Polygon,* April 24, 2015, which stated that the game was slated for release on PC, Mac, Linux, and Ouya, a failed console that was discontinued in the summer of 2015. The game's official website still cites "exact date to be announced." Some articles mentioned iPad and iPhone versions that were planned at some point.

Untitled

THE CENTRAL PROBLEM with the historical study of slavery is its reliance on documents written by the slaver (ship logs), the manager (plantation records), or the master (journals and letters), especially when an algebraic function turns a human into a nonliving number. As with the history of slavery, our knowledge of slave *resistance* is likewise limited by our reliance on documents written by the oppressor, such as wanted ads for fugitive slaves penned by those who would recuperate their "property," contemporary accounts of slave revolts from a biased perspective, and even the occasional mentions found in plantation records. The reduction of human beings to ciphers in a ledger is one issue that scholars like Katherine McKittrick discuss at length. Another is the fact that, if the slave appears in these records, it is most often an indication of violence suffered.[1] How to study these histories without repeating the violence of the reduction of people to statistics is a major concern, and scholars have taken various approaches to address this lack.[2] I would add here that it is equally imperative that we find a way to represent these histories without further commoditizing historically enslaved people by either reducing them to an object of play or an empathy exercise.

1. In "Mathematics Black Life," Katherine McKittrick writes of the "violent arithmetics of the archive" (19): "The asterisked archives are filled with bodies that can only come into being vis-à-vis racial-sexual violence; the documents and ledgers and logs that narrate the brutalities of this history give birth to new world blackness as they evacuate life from blackness" (16).

2. The question of representation and the archive, "its limits, its possibilities, its futures" propels the special issue of the journal *History of the Present* edited by Brian Connolly and Marisa Fuentes. Brian Connolly and Marisa Fuentes, eds., *History of the Present* 6, no. 2 (Fall 2016).

By withholding the subject position of the rebel slave from the player in important ways, such as interrupted immersion, the form of the videogame can acknowledge the broader insufficiency of the historical record. This might be achieved, in other media, by making use of the white space of the canvas, or the blank page, or aural silence, or a narrative gap, or a breakdown in meaning. But here, the medium can underscore the player's separation from the historical subject through its use of false or limited interactivity. I would like to suggest that the videogame is an apt space in which to acknowledge the epistemological gap concerning the historical reality of slave resistance; it points to the insurmountable distance between the historical person and the player.

Digital resources offer a way to contemplate the limits of the archive, the unknowable aspects of enslaved lives that were not recorded, and how society as a whole has been based on the metrics put in place during the transatlantic slave trade. Jonathan Beller writes in *The Message is Murder:*

> what passes today for digital culture (and therefore as a kind of radical break) is actually digital culture 2.0. Global commodification, settler colonialism, the mercantile system, the middle passage, slavery, plantations, and industrial capitalism instantiated a first order digital culture . . . with universalizing aspirations through the globally expansive assignation of quantity to qualities from the early modern period forward.[3]

Beller argues that the digital form is inherently based on the type of data collection achieved in slave ship cargo logs and in plantation account books. The medium of the digital might therefore be the most productive location to wrestle with how digital culture is "built on and out of the material and epistemological forms of racial capitalism, colonialism, imperialism and permanent war" (2). Beller explicitly connects contemporary digital culture to the transatlantic slave trade:

3. Beller, *Message Is Murder,* 5–6.

> In dictating the exact dimensions of the slave ship cargo hold during the middle passage and in pricing the slave on the Mississippi auction block, this digitization of living persons and their qualities lay its representational code upon bodies. Price, it turns out, was a digital message, though not the only one. . . . It shows the convergence of a digital calculus on space, on movement, and on bodies and the ability of this calculus to marginalize or eliminate any sympathetic relation (20).

Productively, the digital form's limitations point not only to the problems with the archive but also to digital culture as the heir of the captain's log, the plantation ledger, and the overseer's labor records: the quantification of people's lives, which coded human beings as commodities.

On the whole, this slim volume has articulated how interactivity is a complex element in depictions of slave revolt. The struggle between the player's control of the digital avatar and the game's resistance of the player—in the challenges he or she must surmount in order to advance the narrative—is redirected to critique not merely the mechanisms of control and resistance to which the enslaved were subjected but also to highlight our own epistemological limitations, as if to say, *we can't win slave resistance; we can't even really know it.*

Narratives about slave resistance should be reevaluated, as the work of understanding our culture's relationship to the history of slavery and resistance and its enduring legacy is all the more urgent in the contemporary political climate. The digital texts that I've presented here use their very form to underscore this quandary: inhabiting the subject position of the historical rebel slave is ultimately bracketed as an impossibility by the games' formal devices. This study has attended to the usefulness of the figurative gap in the middle of these game narratives—whether the aporia is brought about by obstruction, a break in immersion, or an unachievable objective. This study has focused particularly on those moments where the interactivity of the narrative breaks down—interruptions which serve to remind the contemporary player that she is merely playing a game. In that desynchronized space between character and player, these games call into question the stakes of rendering this history *playable*.

In this study, we've examined various formal devices, such as limited interactivity and operationalized weakness, disorienting uses of perspective, and the illusion of choice. We've interrogated the playable character's shifting abilities, the uses of untranslated language in videogames, and aspects of the game that are beyond either the player's or the developer's control, like glitches and fan-shared rumors. We've looked at educational games intended for use in the classroom, mainstream videogames that aim to entertain, and an incomplete videogame that lives only online in demos and the articles that anticipated its ever-deferred release. This last example may be the best embodiment of the digital narrative that withholds itself from the player, stillborn. Just as the historical rebel slave resisted her own commodification, these games (over and above the intentions of the developers) productively refuse to allow the player mastery of the subject.

Acknowledgments

Thanks are due to nearly every member of my department at the University of Tampa for listening, reading, and consulting; to the College of Arts and Letters for financial support and the IT department for tech support; and most importantly, to my undergraduate research assistant, David Restrepo. I am grateful to Stephanie Boluk and Patrick Lemieux for reading suggestions, to Ashley Ferro-Murray for the invitation to present work at the EMPAC Center at Rensselaer University, to Nathan Dize for consultation on my translations, to the designers of *Thralled* for sharing their game demo and to Fulbright for a fellowship to Brazil that enriched my understanding of that game.

(Continued from page iii)

Forerunners: Ideas First

Sarah Juliet Lauro is assistant professor in the department of English and Writing at the University of Tampa. She is coeditor of *Better Off Dead: The Evolution of the Zombie as Posthuman,* author of *The Transatlantic Zombie: Slavery, Rebellion, and Living Death,* and editor of *Zombie Theory: A Reader* (Minnesota, 2017).